Sustainable Compromises

D0763314

The Yurt

Our Sustainable Future

SERIES EDITORS

Charles A. Francis
University of Nebraska–Lincoln

Cornelia Flora
Iowa State University

Tom Lynch
University of Nebraska–Lincoln

Sustainable Compromises

A Yurt, a Straw Bale House,
and Ecological Living

ALAN BOYE

University of Nebraska Press
Lincoln and London

© 2014 by the Board of Regents of the University of Nebraska

∞

Publication of this volume was assisted by a grant from the
Friends of the University of Nebraska Press.

Library of Congress Cataloging-in-Publication Data

Boye, Alan, 1950–
Sustainable compromises: a yurt, a straw bale house, and ecological living / Alan Boye.
pages cm.—(Our sustainable future)
Includes bibliographical references.
ISBN 978-0-8032-6487-8 (paperback: alk. paper)—ISBN 978-0-8032-6502-8 (epub)—
ISBN 978-0-8032-6503-5 (mobi)—ISBN 978-0-8032-6501-1 (pdf) 1. Sustainable living—Vermont.
2. Boye, Alan, 1950—Homes and haunts—Vermont. 3. Ecological houses—Vermont. 4. Ecological
houses—Design and construction. 5. Sustainability—Philosophy. I. Title.
GE198.V5B69 2014
640.28'6—dc23
2013044111

Set in Lyon Text by Renni Johnson.

For Jim Wilson, Jim Exten, and Mollie and Phil Freeman

"The future of all life, including our own, depends
on our mindful steps."
—THICH NHAT HANH, *Essential Writings*

"To those devoid of imagination, a blank place on a map is
a useless waste; to others, the most valuable part."
—ALDO LEOPOLD, *Sand County Almanac*

Contents

_ _ _ _ _ _ _ _

List of Illustrations   xi

1. What I Lived For   1

2. Sustainable Compromises   6

3. Where I Live   13

4. Water   20

5. Design   33

6. Foundations   44

7. El Sol   54

8. Economics   68

9. The Beautiful Tree and Other Disasters   77

10. The Amoeba   87

11. The Straw That Broke The   100

12. Finances   106

13. Collaboration   112

14. Artifacts   125

15. Solitude   133

16. Visitors   141

17. Thick Skin in a Winter of Discontent   147

18. Spring   164

19. Higher Laws   170

20. Postscript: Mistakes Were Made   181

Acknowledgments   187

Notes   189

Bibliography   193

Illustrations

- - - - - - - - -

Frontispiece: The Yurt

1. Linda   xiv

2. The Yurt Toilet   7

3. Tesuque School   69

4. The Tree   83

5. Roof Truss Day   94

6. The Amoeba   94

7. The Author at Work   108

8. Straw House Exterior   121

9. Straw House Interior   123

10. House under Construction   128

11. James C. Wilson at the Yurt   143

12. Exterior Plaster   149

13. Interior Plaster   161

14. Finished House (South View)   183

15. Finished House (North View)   184

Sustainable Compromises

Fig. 1. Linda

1

What I Lived For

In the late spring months of 1973 I built a yurt on a high desert plateau thirty-five miles to the southeast of Santa Fe, New Mexico, and began living there alone. I had just finished teaching fifth grade in the small, mostly Hispanic village of Tesuque. I was almost dead-dog broke, skinny as a rail, and barely twenty-three years old.

I didn't have any idea what to do with my life beyond finding a place where I could live as cheaply as possible. Then friends told me about some land they had found that was for sale for next to nothing. Never mind that it was thirty-two acres covered mostly in cacti and sand or that it was a mile away from the nearest road, never mind that I knew nothing about checking deeds for proper ownership, much less anything about building a structure where a person could survive in such a place—I bought it. Besides, it looked like a good place to try out my self-romanticized vision of the starving artist: some half-crazed genius bent over his cabin's only table, working under the light of a single kerosene lantern, while coyotes howled outside below a pale desert moon.

Soon, with the help of a few friends, I built an odd, cupcake-shaped dwelling on the land. I lived alone there for a little over a year before the rattlesnakes, the loneliness, the black widow spi-

ders in the outhouse, and my own restlessness made me a so-
journer in civilized life again. But for that year, I lived as simply
as a human being could. I lived without running water, electricity, and refrigeration and survived only on the meals I prepared
from a three-month stockpile of canned goods, rice, and beans.
Granted, without my youthful blindness to the fragility of life,
I would never have attempted such an experiment in voluntary
poverty. My regret is that that same youthful blindness prevented
me from properly learning the lessons of that lonely plateau until years later. Once I left the desert, my life became one of modern comforts and conveniences. I forgot nearly everything I had
learned about living simply.

Flash forward thirty-five years. My wife and I had been living
in New England for decades. As we approached retirement age,
we started talking about selling our beautiful but drafty and in-
efficient Victorian house. We wanted a smaller place, one better insulated to withstand Vermont's long cold winters, but also
something we could afford on the modest fixed income we were
anticipating. Wherever we lived, we also wanted it to be as simple and as environmentally sound as possible.

We wore out a couple of real estate brokers trying to find a house
that suited us—the houses were either too far from town or poorly
insulated, either too expensive to fix up or too large. The idea of
building our own home started to grow on us. The more we talked about it, the better it sounded. We decided it was possible to
build a small, inexpensive, and environmentally sound house for
less money than many of the houses we were looking at.

I had been an English teacher for most of my life; I knew next to
nothing about designing a house or about sustainability. I hadn't
thought about such things as the proper depth for a foundation or
the problems of human waste disposal since I lived in the yurt. It
took us three years to build, from our decision to do so until our

first night in the house. The labor was often torturous, brutally hard on both body and spirit. At one point, we were on the brink of financial ruin. At times, our marriage was on very thin ice, and it is a miracle we still have any friends. But—with the help of those friends—we built an off-grid, energy-efficient house, using mostly locally produced materials, and made it a comfortable and affordable dwelling.

Oh, one other thing: the house we built is made of straw.

What I learned from those two attempts at living in better harmony with the world is the subject of this book.

To reach the land where I built the yurt, you drove far into the high, lonely desert south of Santa Fe. The road wound through miles of low, rocky hills the color of straw, speckled with the pale green of piñon and juniper trees. Several desolate miles past the New Mexico State Penitentiary and several desolate miles before you got to my land, you came to a multicolored mailbox with the word "Cornucopia" painted on the side. Three or four couples, an assortment of children under the age of ten, and a handful of dogs, cats, and chickens lived here in a sprawling combination of old adobe buildings, sun-sheltering A-frames, and three or four ramshackle wooden sheds. My friend Bob, who gave me the plans for the yurt, lived at the small commune with his young wife and their infant son. Everyone who lived there shared chores and common space and tried to agree collectively on any issues they faced. Cornucopia survived for only a few years. After a fire destroyed the A-frame, people went their separate ways.

Although I didn't appreciate it at the time, watching how those people tried to work and live together eventually gave me an understanding of both the difficulty and the importance of harmony in human communities. To live with an awareness of the environment isn't simply about using the right light bulb and recycling trash; it also requires that we create communities that can sustain humanity.

One day, shortly after I had moved to the land, I was at Cornucopia. I had volunteered to help replaster one of the commune's adobe buildings. After a mud-speckled day of hard work, all of us were seated in the big common room, eating and drinking from a jug of cheap red wine.

We talked that night about politics, from the local volunteer fire department to the jungles of Vietnam. The world's problems back then were no less disheartening, and we discussed them seriously but with good cheer and friendship.

Someone mentioned how the plaza area of Santa Fe was changing. A multistory hotel was being built and would tower over the old adobe buildings. The place was being transformed from an authentic southwestern town into an "Adobe Disney Land" for tourists.

Bob took a deep hit from the jug. "The problem with the world is that there are too many people," he said. "Plain and simple, that's the gist of it: there are too many people in the world." He handed me the jug. "Of course, living out there at the yurt, you won't see any people at all."

The conversation drifted to talk of my new dwelling. People wanted to know how it was working out. Bob asked whether I was going to install a sod roof, as the plans called for me to do.

He was the one who had seen an item in the *Last Whole Earth Catalog* about a structure that was very inexpensive to build. He sent away for plans for building a yurt, and the plans ended up in my hands. I still have them. In 1973, the year I built the yurt, the average cost of a new home in the United States was $32,000. I don't remember how much it cost me to build the yurt, but last week I took the plans to my friends at a local lumber store. They told me I could build the structure today for only $920, a dirt cheap home even by 1973 standards.

One thing is certain: my decision to build a yurt had little to do with sustainability. I had very little money, and so I decided I was going to find a way to live as cheaply as possible so that I wouldn't have to work at a job. I wasn't going to compromise.

I wasn't smart enough or old enough to accept some kind of middle ground.

2

- - - - - - - - - -

Sustainable Compromises

For several miles past the Cornucopia commune there was nothing but a big empty until the highway came to an old-fashioned, real-life ghost town named Madrid. Madrid consisted of dozens of empty wooden houses, weathered to gray. The houses stood in rows carved into a rocky hillside; rotting curtains hung from open windows. The dry dusty wind tossed tumbleweeds down what once had been its streets. A thriving coal mining town until the early 1950s, when other fuels such as natural gas became cheaper, Madrid had been abandoned for years. Now most of it was on the verge of disappearing.

The highway climbed out of the ghost town toward a small ragged chain of inhospitable peaks: the Ortiz. While I lived at the yurt, their shark-tooth-sharp silhouette was the first thing I saw each morning; and each evening, seated at my campfire, I watched the desert's sunsets turn them pink, then fiery red, then a deep dark blue.

A few miles beyond Madrid, a small faint path wound down from a high shoulder and touched the highway. The road in to the yurt was easy to miss. The pale track doubled back on itself and climbed to a simple gate: two strands of barbed wire stretched between fence posts. You pushed a tight loop of wire off one of the posts and then dragged the two strands of wire out of the way.

Fig. 2. The toilet at the yurt

Once beyond the gate, you bounced across an open plateau. Sharp-needled cholla grew there like weeds. Finally you reached a creaking windmill next to a cow tank full of water. The faint road went on, but that was as close to my land as you could get in a vehicle unless you were willing to drive straight into the juniper and its pin-cushioned, tire-popping cactus.

One brilliant May morning, I drove from Santa Fe in a borrowed pickup. I turned carefully off the highway onto the faint path so as not to spill the load of building supplies piled in the rear of the truck. I parked next to the windmill and began the hard work of hauling supplies to the building site. A few hours later I rested in the shade of a piñon tree. In front of me was a pile of boards, tools, shovels, and one well-used school desk.

Everything I needed to build my first structure: the outhouse.

By the end of that first day, I had dug a four-foot-deep pit in the gnarly jumble of sand and rocks that passed for soil out there. I slept that night in the truck, listening to coyotes howling somewhere up in the Ortiz.

The next day, I hammered together an oddly unique privy, complete with a Dutch door (so if I ever had company, you could sit in privacy but keep the top half of the door open in order to look out to the beautiful expanse beyond). For the toilet I cut a hole in the seat of the school desk. I kept the toilet paper on the desktop.

Although it was not quite as fancy, an outhouse was the first structure I built on our Vermont land as well. I made it in sections in the basement of our Victorian house during the dark cold winter months preceding the summer that we began to build the straw bale house. As soon as the ground thawed in the spring, I hauled the sections out to the land we bought and assembled them over a deep pit. I knew the site would see a lot of use in the coming months, and it would be a long while before we had any other kind of toilet.

If the hole is deep enough, well ventilated, and not near any water source, what better way to take care of human waste than an outhouse? Built correctly, an outhouse doesn't pollute or use any water. In addition, the nasty stuff slowly decomposes and returns important nutrients to the earth.

In other parts of the world human fecal matter is used as a resource. From methane gas for power to high-grade compost, there is a good argument we should not be throwing this shit away. Rose George, in her book *The Big Necessity: The Unmentionable World of Human Waste and Why It Matters*, explains that 90 percent of the world's human waste ends up in the oceans untreated. That sludge contains high amounts nitrogen and phosphates, which help to feed algae. The algae, in turn, suck out the dissolved oxygen in the water, making it uninhabitable for most sea life. On the other hand, that same human waste can produce a useable fuel and makes excellent compost.

Human sewage is classified either as gray water (the not so polluted stuff that goes down the kitchen sink, the shower, and the clothes washer) or as black water (the yucky stuff that gets flushed down the toilet). Gray water can be used to water lawns and gardens with very little treatment, or sometimes none at all.

One day an aging hippie visited our Vermont land. He still lived on a commune he had helped to start decades earlier. It consisted of people who held a common interest in the art of dance. Many of the original members were still living there, while younger ones continue to join. He listened to me trying to figure out the most sustainable sewage system for our new house. He explained that, at the commune where he lived, they just ran gray water into the woods. "What better way to use gray water?" he asked. "All the gray water from the commune goes to keep our woodlot looking healthy. As for the other stuff," he added, "we have composting toilets."

My wife, Linda, and I started to consider having composting toilets in our new Vermont house. We learned that a proper composting toilet does not smell. It has a container that is ventilated so that all odors are removed to the outside. That continuous flow of fresh air speeds up the decomposition process. Unlike the stagnant pit beneath an outhouse, the circulating air in a composting toilet helps to establish a diverse community of microbes, which quickly break down the waste. When a composting toilet is working properly, it produces a dry, fluffy, and odorless compost material. The compost is excellent for flowers and trees, although many authorities do not recommend using it on vegetable gardens.

For a brief moment, it seemed like the perfect plan for our "green" house would be to have a composting toilet and to just run our gray water out into the woods. Simple and renewable.

But . . .

Once, long ago, a gypsy woman read my palm. We sat in a smoky coffee house as she bent over my hand and studied the lines she saw there. After a long pause she said, "You have good ideals, but you will always compromise them." I pulled my hand away, indignant that she could be so wrong; but of course, in time, I knew that she had been correct. Compromise is inevitable in life and—on a planet with six billion people—essential to sustain it.

As times of decisions come to us, our minds conduct a kind of debate weighing the pros and cons of our choices. Sometimes emotions guide us; at other times we turn away from our instincts and choose a less traveled path. But as we age, we come to realize that every choice we make has an impact on others. We may not always make the right decision; but if we realize our impact on others and—dare I say it?—have a set of ideals to live by, the compromises we must make in life will be more sustainable.

Building our house was an ongoing series of such compromises between our green ideals and the more practical matters of time and money.

Take, for example, our decision to build at all. Why create a new structure, when you can use an already existing building? Construction accounts for a significant portion of the depletion of the earth's resources. Even if you have to do a lot to make a used house more efficient, it is almost always less harmful, and less expensive, than building a new one from scratch.

We lived as many twenty-first-century families do: we recycled, tried to conserve on our energy consumption, and shopped around for the most fuel-efficient car. When we decided to downsize and move out of our old Victorian house, we began to think more about how else we might live and use fewer resources. We knew we wanted a place that was small, well built, energy efficient, and cheap to live in. We started looking at houses in the area. Many of them were built when heating fuel was inexpensive and were therefore poorly insulated. We were willing to spend money to make an older house more efficient, but we did have a limit to what we could spend. Once in a great while we would locate a small, well-built home that wouldn't take much to make it more efficient, but we wouldn't like the fact that it was built on a busy street or that it was so far from town.

Eventually, we compromised. We decided to build a new house but to make it as environmentally friendly as possible. This was the first of many decisions where we tried to balance our desire to live more sustainably with our economic, aesthetic, and personal needs.

In 2008, the year we completed our straw bale house, the national average for the cost of a new home was just under $300,000. Although straw is a cheap building material, the cost of labor and other materials, as well as our decision to be off grid, still drove the cost of our small three-bedroom home to $150,000, or to half the average price for a new home. On the other hand, because it is so efficient, our house is very inexpensive to maintain. We heat with wood; and since straw is such a good insulator, heating the house costs us next to nothing. If I did not cut my own wood for free, our annual heating bill would be about $350.

We use propane gas for some of our appliances. Propane is certainly not renewable, and its production and transportation is anything but sustainable. But our consumption averages out to only 20 gallons a month, or 240 gallons a year. Although prices will inevitably rise, this currently means we spend about $50 a month on propane. With a little research, we found the most energy-efficient clothing washer and dryer available. They are small but big enough for the two of us. On nice days we dry our clothes outside.

In addition to the dryer and the water heater, we use propane for our cooking. I considered installing a modern version of the old-fashioned wood-burning cookstove, but they are not cheap. They heat up the interior of a house during the summer months and require more physical labor than I thought I would have in my later years. In the end, I decided such a stove was not practical for us.

We installed solar panels for electricity; so when the sun is shining, our electricity is free. But the area where I live has the lowest number of sunny days in the continental United States. During the especially dark months of November and December, I make up for the lack of sunshine by using a gasoline powered generator once every two or four days to charge the electrical system's set of large storage batteries. In an average year we use sixty-five gallons of gasoline for the generator.

Because the house is so energy efficient, only a small portion of our yearly budget is subject to the ever-increasing cost of fossil fuels. Our expenses stay about the same from month to month. That means, so far anyway, the straw bale house has lived up to one of the key goals we set: affordability.

While we were making these decisions about our future home, the State of Vermont passed new wastewater laws. In them were provisions for composting toilets, but to be legal we would have to treat our human compost as a dangerous pathogen and bury it. Also, the new law still would require us to put in a septic system just to treat our gray water. The tipping point came when we realized that most composting toilets use electricity to circulate fresh air. That conflicted with our hope of significantly reducing our use of energy.

So we compromised and chose to have conventional toilets.

3

Where I Live

Knowing we would have flush toilets meant that wherever we built our new house, the land would have to accommodate a septic system and its leach field. We also wanted land that was close to town so that we could easily get to stores, the theater, the library, and the hospital. The problem was that we couldn't afford land that was very close, yet we wanted to reduce our dependency on our car. We drew a ten-mile radius around the town and decided we would try to find a place within that area. We picked ten miles hoping that we could find land that was affordable yet close enough that we could sometimes ride our bicycles to town.

Using those requirements as a start, we began to develop a list of rules for a house site. In addition to being within our budget, no more than ten miles from town, and able to accommodate a septic system, the place had to have good southern exposure, be close to good roads, and have enough space for a large vegetable garden. Even though Vermont is known for its calendar-quality views, it wasn't very important to us that the house site have a good view. We also didn't care about how few or many acres, only about how useable and affordable any potential land might be.

Over the course of about a year, we looked at several pieces of land. We found a few that came close to what we wanted. We visited those over and over again trying to determine if they would work for us.

We kept looking at a thirteen-acre plot that had the distinction of being the cheapest land within ten miles of town. It had good southern exposure, as well as other advantages, but it had one major flaw: it was on a hillside so steep that putting in a driveway was going to cost a mint. We nicknamed it the Heliport because we joked that we would need a chopper to access our house site.

One Sunday we drove out to the Heliport for another look. We inspected the woods. They were mostly softwoods, spruce and white pine, but with a good smattering of hardwoods mixed in. They would make a sufficient woodlot for fuel. We climbed up the slope and found the remnants of a small cabin near its peak. The spot was level enough for a building site but would require a long, steep drive. We made our way down the slope until we found another site that was somewhat lower.

We climbed down the hill and stood at the bottom. We studied the hillside, trying to visualize how a drive might snake its way up to the site, when we heard someone call out.

"You really interested in that land?"

We turned. A stocky man with a pleasant face was making his way up the road. "My name's Alan Fogg," he said. "My wife and I live just over there." He pointed. Through the woods, we could see his house. "Are you guys interested in that land?"

"We are," I answered.

He nodded. "I'll sell you this adjoining land for the same price. It's not as many acres, but it's better land."

He described the boundaries of the property. I left Linda chit-chatting with him and took off into the woods, following his description of the property's boundaries. With every step, it became clearer that we had found our land. I discovered at least three decent house sites. I could tell that the woodlot was much better here. Good, long-burning fuels like maple, beech, and oak grew on a gradual, south-facing slope. There was plenty of room for a garden. It was close enough to town. There was only one unanswered question.

"I have to be sure we can put in a septic," I said when I got back.

Alan Fogg smiled. "Oh, you'll be able to put in a septic."

"If I can . . ." I stuck out my hand, "then you've got a deal."

We shook.

Linda spoke slowly, as if coming out of a dream. She looked at me. "Did we just buy some land?"

On the drive home I assured her this was the right place. Because we knew what we needed and had seen so many parcels, I knew that this land came closest to meeting all our conditions. The only drawback was that—at nine miles—the land was at the extreme of our "less than ten miles from town" rule.

Finding out if we could have a septic system took a couple of weeks. We had to hire a man with an excavator to poke holes in the ground, and we had to hire a septic engineer to test those holes to make sure they could serve as a leach field. During that time, we discovered a small brook that tumbled down from the Heliport and bisected the property. The stream ran through the heart of the land, a tiny silver thread winding its way through the stifling green of the towering woods. The stream made for a nice feature, and it also opened up the possibility of putting in a small hydroelectric system for some of our electricity.

Although we are nine miles from town, we are only three miles from a couple of small and beautiful New England villages. Each village boasts a few properly painted white steeples, and centuries-old houses framed by quaint picket fences. Each has a small store selling groceries and simple hardware. One store sells gasoline as well. The stores also serve as impromptu meeting halls for the community of friends and neighbors.

While we waited for the results of the septic tests, I visited the town offices in order to make sure there were no problems with the deed. That was at least one lesson I had learned from my experience with the yurt.

Look, one thing that should be clear by now is that any unemployed, broke, twenty-three-year-old who was building a yurt smack dab in the middle of nowhere might be the same kind of twenty-three-year-old who wouldn't have cared or known much about silly things like ownership and deeds. If I had cared, however, I might have discovered that I was "buying" the land from a man who did not own it.

In 1770, at about the same time people named Carrick and Gilfillan and Warden were coming to this part of Vermont from Scotland, Mexican citizens were petitioning the Spanish government for land in the new world. It was common for the Spanish government to reward former soldiers with large tracts of land. In fact, the New Mexico land where I built my yurt had been granted to a Mexican soldier.

Or . . . maybe not. It wasn't clear.

The area where I built the yurt was unoccupied in 1848, when the United States acquired jurisdiction over it as a result of the Mexican-American War. Problems soon arose regarding who owned the large land grant. Claims by Mexican descendants conflicted with those of Texas cattlemen. Mix those problems with politics, throw in unscrupulous lawyers and a gold rush in the Ortiz Mountains, and you get some idea of the difficulty of determining the ownership of my New Mexico land.

I had built the yurt and was living there, but the man I was buying the land from had not produced the deed. I continued to make payments on the land even after I abandoned living at the yurt. Each time I tried to clarify who actually owned the land, the man led me on a wild goose chase. An expensive lawyer I hired told me it could take years and a lot of money and even then it might never be clear who really had title to that land. He suggested I simply stop making payments and walk away. In the end, I took his advice. Still, I consider those monthly $79 payments a pretty cheap price for my year-long experiment in living.

As I traced the genealogy of the Vermont land, in order not to make the same kind of mistake again, we crawled all over those ten acres trying to decide where we might build. My initial impressions about the property proved to be correct. There were three places to build a house. We quickly eliminated one for a variety of reasons. We had the other two tested and learned that either would support a septic system.

One of the sites was in the center of the property. The very secluded spot gave us the delightful feeling of being deep in the Vermont woods, with not a human artifact in sight. The other site was near a road. A smaller area and not nearly as private, it did have the advantage of having utility poles close at hand, and it would require a shorter driveway.

We couldn't decide. We needed help.

There ensued the initial employment of the Amoeba—a nebulous network of kind and generous friends and relatives who would continue to be on our unpaid payroll for the duration. The Amoeba's work began at once. Time after time we would drag friends out to the land and walk them from one site to the other while babbling about our concerns like schoolchildren. They would listen and nod, offer advice and point out things we hadn't thought about. One beautiful early autumn day, we were tramping through the woods with two friends, when the man turned to us and said, "The one in the center of the land, that's the artist's site." I perked up with that old false pride—just like the yurt! "And the other one," he said, "the other one is the accountant's site."

Ah yes . . . money. The downside of the "artist's site" was that it was farther from the road. That would mean that it would cost

more to bring in power and that we'd have to build a longer driveway. I got bids on how much each driveway might cost, and the
power company sent out a man who helped me figure out how
much extra it would cost to bring power to the centrally located site.

But the more we looked at that site, the clearer its advantages
were. The area was larger, which meant we could have a good-sized
garden; and while it would mean a longer driveway, the access to it
was from a paved road, whereas access to the "accountant's site"
was from a dirt road. That would make a difference during Vermont's long muddy spring.

We began to explore using solar power. Although solar power systems are expensive, you can limit their cost by designing a
home and living in such a way as to minimize the use of electricity.

We knew that if we were going to build with environmental
awareness, we had to carefully consider *every* decision we made:
from which building site to use to energy efficiency to aesthetics.
That part was easy, but we also had to take a closer look at our
own lifestyle and how we might be able to change it. Corny as it
sounds, I began to chant the hackneyed phrase "leave a smaller
footprint" as our mantra.

That doesn't mean I was willing to return to the extreme lifestyle of the yurt, but the same desire to simplify my life seemed to
be at the center of both houses. Simplicity, as Henry David Thoreau noticed, allows you to see the world around you clearer and
allows you to live a more fulfilled life. Simplicity, as his pal Ralph
Waldo Emerson asserted, also allows you to experience life more
directly. My life at the yurt was so simple that, much of the time,
I was bored; but because of that simplicity, I saw the living world
around me as no other time in my life.

I'll admit that nostalgia for those times might have pushed me
to choose the artist's site, rather than the accountant's, for our Vermont home. In the end, the decision to build an off-grid house at

the artist's site might have had as much to do with wild turkeys as with anything else. One early spring day just before we made the final choice, I was walking alone through the Vermont woods. Gray stately maples towered above me, their crowns already reddening with buds. I was looking up at them while I bushwhacked down the slope toward the secluded artist's building site. I barely glanced as I stepped over a fallen tree.

The explosion nearly took off my head.

A brown cannonball burst into flight, her gobbles like some Cheyenne warrior's call. I looked down. I had nearly stepped on a nest of a dozen turkey eggs. The mother had waited until the last possible moment to fly. Directly in front of me was the level area where a house might sit.

I broke out of the woods and stood in the warming light of the spring sun, imagining how we might live just here.

4

- - - - - - - -

Water

Although he never lived extravagantly, Henry Thoreau chose to live in poverty for two years at Walden Pond. He wanted to see just how little one really needed to live a comfortable life. More than comfort, Thoreau was interested in freeing himself from the slavery of spending all his time working just in order to live.

He made a list of the absolute necessities, those things "so important to human life that few, if any, whether from savageness, or poverty, or philosophy, ever attempt to do without." He boiled down his list to just four items: food, shelter, clothing, and fuel. He examined each of those in order to determine how little a person really needed in order to live comfortably and, most importantly, to still allow free time to read and think, or just look around.

He spent a great deal of time contemplating the economy of owning property and building a house. He explored the necessity of keeping warm, of clothing, and of being able to feed oneself and one's family without having to work endless hours.

During his two-year experiment at Walden, Thoreau raised beans that he sold to pay for the rest of his food. He kept meticulous records of every penny coming and going and wrote about his diet of bread, rice, beans, peas, potatoes, pork, sweet potatoes, sugar, fish caught from the pond, and, as one of several "experiments which failed" one woodchuck.

While admonishing his fellow New Englanders for their needless extravagance in food and shelter, he never mentions water except to acknowledge it, along with food, as a necessity. Nowhere in his financial listing, and seldom in his day-to-day activities, does he write about water.

Naturally, Thoreau took his water from Walden Pond, just as his neighbors used local streams and springs or dug wells for their water. In dry years some of these sources disappeared, but as a rule water was never much of an expense in the budget of nineteenth-century Americans. In a very un-Thoreau-like way, Thoreau took the availability of water for granted, concentrating instead on how little it cost him to have a sufficient and healthy diet.

As the crow flies, our land in Vermont is only 150 miles from Walden Pond. We live in a part of the world where winter snowpack often exceeds thirty feet deep. Everywhere there are lakes and ponds. Take a walk in the woods, and you'll find springs bubbling up in mossy, rocky pools.

> Water, water everywhere,
> And all the boards did shrink;
> Water, water everywhere,
> Nor any drop to drink.

In the Vermont town where we lived before building our straw bale house, drinking water comes from a reservoir a few miles from the village. Water runs from the man-made lake into a small filtration plant and from there downhill through pipes to a large water tank built onto a hillside outside town. Gravity feeds the water down to our old house. Four times a year the town sends out a bill for this and for sewer service.

There are a few problems with this system. Many people, for example, filter the town water because of particulates and, to some, an unpleasant taste. The pipes between the reservoir and the town's residences are old, and sections are replaced only when they break. To ease the amount of residue in the water, town workers go each spring from one fire hydrant to another. Kids and adults gather around to witness the annual event. The workers open the hydrant and let the water pour out onto the street. At first, a sickly orange-red fluid more like blood than water storms out with an astounding force. The tainted water splashes onto the pavement, driving a torrent of last autumn's dry leaves down the street. After ten minutes or so, the water begins to run clear. Using a wrench the size of a baseball bat, the workers shut off the water and then drive down the street to the next hydrant. For the next day or so, our water would have a faint reddish tint to it.

The town's reservoir is fed by a number of small brooks that drain an increasingly populated area. A state highway passes along one side, and generally people heed the signs that read, "Public Water Source. No fishing. No swimming. No boats." More problematic might be the interstate highway that passes by the reservoir's entire length just two hundred yards away. As the interstate was being built, some people argued it shouldn't be placed so close to the town's water. They noted that if there were to be an accident involving a truck carrying toxic liquids, it might permanently affect the town's water supply. The highway was built anyway. To date, there have not been any accidents involving tanker trucks near the pond.

I put in a filtering system at our old Victorian house. Twice a year I changed the filter, a frustrating job that involved coaxing the device open with a plastic wrench and being soaked by water draining back on me. Before I tossed the old filter, I studied how dark and clogged it had become.

One day fifty years ago my mother stood at our kitchen sink. She ran the faucet to get the water good and cold and then filled her glass. She drank the water slowly but without stopping. She set the glass down and watched me watching her. Then, as was often the case with her, she made a prediction about the future: "Good-tasting water is going to disappear. One day people will have to pay a lot of money for a drink like I just had."

She was right, of course. A recent United Nations report states that the United States is the largest consumer of bottled water in the world. It reports that bottled water is not sustainable and points out that 17 million barrels of oil are consumed by the U.S. bottled-water market alone. Many environmentalists note that much of our bottled water is simply tap water put into bottles and sold. Others say that the marketing of bottled water makes people think there is something wrong with their tap water, when in fact that may not be the case.

Clearly there is a problem with the amount of potable water that is available in the world. In addition to a lack of drinking water, aquifers that have existed for thousands of years are drying up, having been tapped for irrigation and other uses. The populations of large western U.S. cities located in areas with limited water resources have exploded in the last few decades, making the legal, ethical, and moral questions of water rights critical for the future.

I never thought about any of that while living at the yurt; I just knew that once or twice a week I needed to refill my water supply. On days when there was the slightest breeze and I knew the windmill would be pumping fresh water, I grabbed two green plastic five-gallon containers and headed off to the windmill. At first there wasn't much of a path, but after a month or two I'd worn a faint tread on the desert floor. I walked the half mile through isolated piñon and juniper, always keeping one eye out for rattlesnakes. Ear-piercing whistles came from strange desert insects hiding amid the rabbitbrush. Except for the howl of a coyote, no other sound is as sweet on that beautiful landscape.

Often I took my time, exploring new areas of the desert as I went; but eventually I reached the windmill.

That old windmill was a marvelous device. All across the West, the once-ubiquitous wooden paddlewheel windmill made it possible to pump water for livestock in remote places using just the wind. As the blades twirled in the wind, they raised and lowered the handle on an old-fashioned pump. Squeaking and wheezing like some terminal asthmatic, the pump sloshed a steady stream of cool water into large tanks for livestock to use. The availability of electricity and the use of high-volume pumps have made the old wooden windmills all but extinct.

Although there hadn't been cattle on that part of New Mexico for a decade, the windmill still worked. The water poured from the pump and spilled into a low, metal tank. Luckily, the tank still held water.

Most days when I got to the windmill, I stripped and—careful not to cut myself on the metal—climbed into the tank. The bottom was an oozing thick blanket of slime, but the sudden shock of ice-cold water against my desert-parched skin made it all worth it. I scrubbed my body, splashed at imaginary playmates (it got mighty lonely out there on the desert), and floated on my back, content to do nothing but stare into the empty New Mexican sky.

In time to the turning of the blades came a rhythmic creaking of wood and metal and of man-made things no longer in need of men's ears. I felt like a thief, come to steal back the glory of some timeless West.

I would climb slowly out of the tank, loath to leave the cool comfort of the only water for miles in any direction. I soaked my shirt in the tank before putting it on, the wet covering serving as a personal air conditioner for the long, hard walk back to the yurt.

Then I turned to the work before me: getting my supply of water. I filled each container directly from the pump, took a deep breath, and then picked them up for the trek back to the yurt.

A gallon of water weighs 8.3 pounds. I never filled the containers all the way; but even so, I had to transport at least seventy pounds back across the burning sands of the desert. I carried a five-gallon container in each hand, stopping every hundred yards or so to catch my breath and give my muscles a break. Before I had gone a quarter of the way back, any remnant of my cool bath had vanished, and my shirt was bone dry. My arms ached, and my head swirled in the intense heat and unblinking strength of the sunlight. For hours after I got the two containers all the way back home, my arms seemed like spent rubber bands.

I had purchased the two plastic containers for my water at some 1970s edition of the Big Box Store. The containers were built to last. I can prove it, because somehow one of those containers has managed to follow me through the now nearly forty years and the dozens of times I have moved since then. I found uses for it along the way and use it still at the straw bale house to carry water to my upper garden. After the whirlwind of house construction was completed, I began to reflect on how the old plastic container had survived all these years. It seems impervious to decomposition. Despite its life baking in desert sunlight and forty subsequent years of use and aging, the container shows no signs of wear. On the other hand, a five-gallon container I purchased when I started building the straw bale house literally fell apart in its third year. I was astounded at the longevity of my old container, but "back then" there was no concern about how long human-made objects might remain in the environment.

Timothy Morton, a professor of literature and the environment at UC Davis, calls materials that will last an unfathomable amount of time "hyperobjects." They include plastics, radioactive materials like plutonium, Styrofoam, and other man-made materials. In "Hyperobjects and the End of Common Sense," Morton argues that "Hyperobjects stretch out ideas of time and space since they far outlast most human time scales, or they're massively distributed in terrestrial space and so are unavailable to immediate experience." Many of these objects are being absorbed into our bodies and the environment; but we fail to comprehend them, because they are "beyond our normal scope of imagination."

Any talk of sustainability has to include a frank acknowledgment of the future of hyperobjects and the delayed destruction that they disperse across time and space. These are so unknown, so anonymous, and, because they "far outlast most human time scales," so indifferent to the sensationalized immediacy of our image-driven world. If my old green container looks as good as new after forty years, then tens of millions of its mates, to say nothing of the tens and millions of other man-made objects, remain indefinitely in landfills or oceans or on high desert plains once unspoiled by such debris. We occupy a minute speck of time and space, and yet we are leaving toxins that will not disappear even after humankind itself has vanished. We must shift our vision of the future from the immediate survival of our species to a far more expansive scale.

One lesson that my year on the desert taught me was never to take water for granted.

Or at least, that was the lesson I thought I had learned.

It is difficult to imagine any two places in the continental United States that are more opposite than my New Mexican desert and these Vermont hills. Take simple geography, for example. The Internet informs me that my straw bale house is 1,901.8 miles from the ruins of the yurt (still visible on satellite images). The average rainfall in Vermont is nearly five times that of the high deserts south of Santa Fe. In addition, surface water is much more available in Vermont's abundance of ponds, streams, and rivers.

Despite its apparent profusion, water is a concern in Vermont. Like most other people building in rural areas, we had to drill a well for water. Drilling a well is not cheap, and it is always a gamble. You never know how deep you will have to drill to get potable water, and drilling companies charge based on how deep they have to go.

Vermont, like many other states, provides maps that show the depths of most water wells. However, the data wasn't much help. The information was nearly a decade old, and the depths of those wells ranged from eighty-five to four hundred feet, making it difficult to accurately estimate the cost. The going rate for drilling was $26 a foot, and we would need another two grand just for the pump and pressure tank.

Before we could get a loan to build, the bank required an itemized cost estimate for the house. Since we didn't have any way of knowing how deep the well might have to be, coming up with a number was a crapshoot. But we needed water, and that meant we had to drill until we hit some or ran out of money trying.

As it turned out, drilling a well gave us our first full-frontal view into the abyss of financial disaster.

I hired a local man to drill our well. I met him one autumn day not long after our driveway was finished. John Ainsworth was the kind of man you like right away. He hopped out of his truck, smiled broadly, and extended his hand. We walked the area where I wanted to build. The well had to be one hundred feet away from the house and its septic system. John soon found a good spot where it would be easy to get the drilling rig in.

"Any guess how deep we might have to go?" I asked.

John shrugged and then went back for something in his truck. When he returned, he held out a pair of wires that were joined together at one end. "I don't know how you feel about dowsing," he said. "I don't trust it myself, but . . ." He took the loose ends of the wires in each hand and flipped their joined ends straight up.

"You know how to dowse?"

He was already walking over the area we had selected for the well. "Anyone can do it," he began, but he then drew silent as he moved about. In a moment, the tip of the wires flipped down. John took a step back and tried it again. Same result. "Two hundred and fifty feet," he said.

"You can tell how deep it is?"

John shrugged again. He moved left and right and then came back to the spot. As if pulled by phantom fingers, the wires dipped again at the ground. "You got a rock or something to mark this spot with?"

If you had asked me the day before, I would have told you there was no way you could predict the location and depth of water by flipping a couple of wires or twigs in your hands, but by that evening I had convinced myself we would hit water by 250 feet.

A week later I met John and his drilling crew at the land. I didn't think the truck carrying the pipe would make it down the drive, much less the drill rig itself. The rig came on a large truck bed driven by a man who looked like he'd driven it into worse places.

I watched them set things up, but soon I had to go to work. John jotted down my work phone number. "Just in case," he said.

Several hours later I was talking to a student writer about an essay she had written, when the phone in my office rang. It was John; they were at four hundred feet.

"Four hundred feet?" I shouted.

My student sprang up and made her way toward the door. "I'll come back," she said, and disappeared.

"Yes, afraid so," he said. "But the rock is changing, and that is a good sign."

"Sign?"

"I say we go another twenty-five feet and see what we have."

By the time I left work that day, our well was 425 feet deep. There was water, but not much. John said he needed to let the well sit, and then he'd be able to tell us more.

I had already determined how much water the two of us required in a day. Using a water budget I calculated how much water we needed for toilets, showers, washing machines, and a garden. We never use a dishwasher, and we were going to install very low-flush toilets. I felt pretty smug when we only totaled forty-five gallons a day.

Then, a week later, John called again. Our 425-foot-deep well was only yielding a trickle of water. What was worse was that the static level was at 325 feet, meaning we only could store 150 gallons in the well itself before the water seeped back into the ground. If we used the water too quickly, we would have to wait for the well to fill again.

I never thought I would see the day when the mossy old cow tank near the yurt would seem like a luxury to me, but it held nearly three times as much water as our well would. Not only was the cow tank much larger, but the windmill brought a steady stream of cool, clear water to the surface of the desert using the power of the wind alone. Now, here I was, stuck in Vermont—the French didn't call them the GREEN mountains for nothin'—with barely a drop to drink.

John advised us to wait until spring.

"And then?"

He hesitated, "Then you could try a different spot." Even through the phone, he probably heard my chin crash onto the floor. "But try not to worry. We'll come back in the spring and measure it again. If there's no change, we could hydrofrack before we do anything else."

Hydrofracking is short for "hydraulic fracturing," a process where liquid is forced down a well under intense pressure in order to increase the size and number of the natural fractures in the rock. When it works, these new and wider fractures can increase the flow of water or, in the case of the oil industry, petroleum and gas. In large scale operations, the process has caused a number of problems, from contaminating drinking water supplies to possibly increasing earthquake activities. A small hydrofracking job on my 425-foot-deep well would be done with water, not chemicals as is often the case in the oil industry. But frankly, I didn't think much about the environmental risks; instead, I fretted over the additional cost and the possibility that even after the hydrofracking, the well might still not provide enough water.

All winter long I stewed over our water situation. My very first obstacle—the lack of enough water—seemed to derail the entire project of living on less. We could not afford to spend much more money on the well without having to cut the budget in other places. We could be sinking so much money into a well that we wouldn't have enough left to build the house. On the other hand, the well we had so far would barely give us the minimum water we needed. What made it worse was that, by then, we were nearly full force into the project. We had already started the process of listing our house with a realtor and had just taken out a construction loan from the bank.

"Simplify!" Hank Thoreau shouts. But how?

I worked that winter designing the final plans for the house. I continued to get bids and look for local sources of building materials. I talked to contractors, designers, architects, bankers, carpenters, plumbers, and electricians. I walked the building site and planted apple trees and grapes. But no matter how busy I was, the situation with the well was always on my mind. It was the first of many periods of deep doubt and despair.

One of the aspects of the straw house was that it would have two drains to wick water away from the foundation, instead of a single drain found in a traditional house. Our second drain would carry the roof water away from the house. I chewed on this fact for a while and saw a way to take care of some of our water needs. I would direct the water from this second drain into a cistern. I could install a small pump, powered by its own tiny solar panel, to pump this water for the garden, which would reduce our summertime water needs.

John returned in the spring to discover there was still only a trickle of water in the well, and we had no choice but to hydrofrack. One morning, the drilling rig returned with a water tanker close behind. They set up the equipment, and then the men blasted water down my well. They pulled everything out, and then John took some measurements. A miracle of sorts happened, as the well had gone from a trickle to a rush, thanks to the hydrofracking. We had water, and plenty of it. I had already installed the cistern; but after the success of the hydrofracking, I didn't need it for water. Eventually I was able to convert the cistern for use as our root cellar.

Even though we have plenty of water now, I no longer take it for granted. I am considerably more careful about my water use than in those days on the desert. Back then the only expenditure was in the energy it took me to carry those heavy containers all the way back to the yurt. I limited my use not because I had decided or needed to live with less but because I was lazy.

Although a thorough and hard worker, Thoreau himself spent a good bit of time at Walden lazing around the pond. He did not consider living with less as a hardship but rather as a way to give himself more time to pursue the higher purposes in life: close observation of the world and contemplation of his place in it. Initially my ordeal with the well did not make my life simpler; and even though we have plenty of water now, we use it carefully so as to not squander this resource. This awareness has not so much gained us free time but instead, in a very Thoreau-like way, has provided us an opportunity for a constant contemplation of the necessities of life and of how mindful we must be of those gifts.

5

Design

There is no way around it; in building either a house or a life there's going to be compromise. "While I'd like to build the perfect house," Sam Clark writes, in his book *Independent Builder: Designing and Building a House Your Own Way*, "it makes more sense to me to design and build the pretty-efficient, largely non-toxic, mildly re-cycled, partially timbered, semi-great house."

I learned a lot from his book. He writes about the use of "pat-tern languages" in designing a beautiful, comfortable, and useful home. The idea is to have a list of simple rules and to apply them as patiently and consistently as possible. Instead of deciding "I want a ranch style home" and designing something from there, you make a list of the characteristics that are common to human history's most beautiful, functional, and comfortable buildings. You then create a set of design rules based on those characteris-tics. These rules cover such things as indoor sunlight, passage-ways, ceiling height, and interior walls. In this way, you begin to design your house based on what works, what is beautiful, and how you live. The style of the house evolves, rather than having been chosen from the outset.

An example could be making the common, more "public" spac-es in a small house as large as possible; if the common area feels large, then the entire house will feel large as well. One good way to make the public room seem even larger is by having a lot of windows that provide sunlight and a nice view.

Voila! Our small house would have a large public room with south-facing windows.

Instead of thinking about what we wanted the finished house to look like, we designed our house from the inside out. This way of thinking led us to study the way Linda and I lived and how we wanted to live. As a result we knew our house would have quiet personal spaces where we could get away and be alone. We decided, because of our advancing age, we wanted to make our house wheelchair accessible as well.

I began to apply a set of principles that would help to guide me in every decision:

Make it simple—simple to build and simple to live in. Simplicity gives a structure its beauty.

Make it integrated. The house's structural elements should serve multiple goals such as passive solar heating, natural lighting, insulation, and so on.

Make it energy efficient, inexpensive to maintain, easy to build, and durable.

And at every stage of design and construction, I should consider both the long-term and short-term environmental implications of every decision.

As I was slowly figuring out what kind of house we would build, I explored the land we had chosen as a building site. Any free moment would find me scrambling through young beech trees, their whiplike branches slapping against my arms, or whacking through weeds and brambles. I carried an old-fashioned compass and tape measure, taking measurements as I moved over the land. At night I drew crude topographical scale maps of the area on big sheets of freezer paper. I used these to help me envision where exactly to put a modest-sized house that took the best advantage of natural sunlight.

I hired experts to evaluate the land: foresters to tell me about the woodlot, excavators and septic builders, carpenters and concrete workers. As we walked the site together, I scribbled their advice in a notebook.

One cool day I stood at the site, with a stocky, good-natured man named Harold. He was a concrete contractor and was sizing up the site for me. I wanted his opinion about the cost and difficulty of getting concrete trucks in and out and what it might take to put in a foundation. I told him I was interested in building a sustainable home, and he perked up.

"You could build with ICFs," he said.

I was trying to decode the acronym when Harold helped me.

"Insulated Concrete Forms," he said. He explained a system of building using box-shaped frames that are later filled with concrete. The frames are made of polystyrene, an efficient insulation. Like some kid with a set of Legos, you stack the blocks to create the perimeter wall. Once they are filled with concrete, they create a very energy-efficient wall, solid enough to support the roof. The building system uses very little wood, and it goes up quickly. It is cost-efficient and makes a beautiful structure. Harold had never built one but had gone to seminars about them and was willing to try.

For a while, I considered Harold's ICF building system, but it didn't meet enough of my rules. For one thing, polystyrene is not a very sustainable building material. More importantly, however, the manufacture of concrete uses an incredible amount of resources. Concrete is made of several raw ingredients that are ground together to make a powder and then put in a kiln with zones that progressively heat the powder to a temperature of 2,700°F (1,480°C). According to *Environmental Building News*, six-tenths of 1 percent of the total energy consumption in the United States is from the manufacture of concrete. Worse yet, the worldwide production of cement accounts for over 8 percent of all carbon-dioxide emissions from human activities.

Although I rejected the ICF system, Harold's knowledge and enthusiasm led me to learn more about other alternative building systems. I talked to people who had built log houses and timber frame houses, adobe houses and stone houses, earthships made with old automobile tires and cob houses sculpted from a mixture of straw and mud. I learned about underground houses, houses made from cord wood, and houses built with food cans filled with dirt.

I already knew about straw bale buildings. I grew up in Nebraska, where the world's first straw bale buildings were constructed well over a hundred years ago. I'd even seen a few of them in my travels in the western part of the state. I knew many of them were still standing, apparently no worse for wear.

In 1863, in order to populate the sparse western lands, Congress passed the Homesteading Act, which gave anyone who would live on it 160 acres in the American West. By 1900 all the best land had been taken. What remained were treeless, sometimes waterless open ranges not suitable for small-scale farming. A group of Nebraska cattlemen petitioned their U.S. Congressman to sponsor legislation that would allow homesteaders to claim much larger tracts of land, up to 1,280 acres instead of just 160. When the act passed in 1904, a second pioneer movement began. The men and women who briefly flocked to the Sand Hills of western Nebraska hoping for a new life found next to nothing to build with: everywhere they looked was sand hill after golden sand hill held down by a windswept sea of grass. Machines had recently been invented that could compress straw and hay and tie it into small rectangular bales. Settlers, looking for building supplies, made a logical choice. Using those bales for construction was a natural fit. Although the oldest known straw bale structure is an 1886 Ne-

braska schoolhouse, these latter-day pilgrims to the Sand Hills ac-
counted for the first boom in straw bale construction. The Sand
Hill pioneers used straw bales to build houses and barns, church-
es and bunkhouses. Now straw bale construction can be found in
countries all over the world.

The more I learned about straw bale construction, the better
it seemed to fit our goals. It certainly met our hopes for building
with sustainable materials. Also, it has great insulating value, is
more fire resistant than many other "standard" building materials, and is quite durable if built correctly. One of the oldest re-
maining Nebraska straw bale buildings, a ranch house built in
1905, remains in excellent condition.

As with any building material, there were also possible compromises. While rodents in a well-built straw house aren't a problem (though hay contains seed heads that attract them, straw does
not), moisture can be. The bales will rot if not kept dry. Cracks in
the plaster, ground water, even years of using poorly ventilated
bathrooms can affect the structure.

What eventually sold me on a straw building (aside from the
admitted irrationality of my Nebraska-native pride) was how well
it met my list of guiding principles.

As we were deciding whether or not to build with straw, my wife
and I visited other straw bale houses in our area. Although they are
a long way from common in Vermont, there were over sixty-five
straw bale homes in the state in 2007. We visited an elegant three-
bedroom home in southern Vermont and another beautiful home
of a young couple not more than three miles from our house site.

Oddly enough, directly across the road from that second house
another young couple built yet another straw bale house. Theirs
was the most basic house we had seen. It was a single large room
supported by beautiful exposed wood beams the owner had cut
from trees in his woods. Several years earlier, these hearty young

folks, "homesteaders," as they call themselves, had disposed of almost all their belongings; and with the money, they purchased a few acres on a south-facing hill. For the first year, they lived in a canvas tent. They had nothing beyond the essentials for survival: a small woodstove, pots and pans, tools.

From the outset, they understood they would need more (there is nothing sustainable about spending Vermont winters in a canvas tent), but they agreed they would only add items to their life if they deemed them an absolute necessity. The following summer, they built a tiny one-room log cabin from wood they harvested and milled by themselves. A couple of years later, after their son was born, they built their four hundred-square-foot straw bale house. They connected the straw house to the log cabin, which now serves as a kitchen and pantry.

The first thing we noticed as we approached their house was how unobtrusive it was. A small pale-white building sat snugged up against a hillside. The soft grayish white of the plastered house blended into the landscape. The corners of the house were slightly rounded, giving it a soft feel. Unlike wood houses, straw bale houses have no sharp edges.

Straw bale construction is similar to building with adobe. The bales are thick, like adobe bricks, and allow for deep-set doors and windows. Just like the old haciendas in New Mexico, straw bale houses are covered with adobe plaster.

Despite its small size, the inside of the house felt spacious. The handcrafted wooden beams that supported the roof were exposed at either end of the room. There was a big table and comfortable places to sit. Hand-hewn window sills let in light that filled the entire house. Although the homesteaders' straw house looked lived-in, the space was not cluttered. There were a few books, a few kids' toys, and, in the walkway that connects the house to the log-cabin kitchen, jars of produce from the garden.

The care and beauty in making the house was astounding, but what was even more impressive was how uncompromising these two people have been in their decision to live simply and sustainably.

I didn't have such admirable goals when I was young and lived at the yurt; rather, I was influenced by a more romantic, less pragmatic ideal. I grew up reading the nature essays of writers like Thoreau, Loren Eiseley, Anne Morrow Lindbergh, and Colin Fletcher. The summer I built the yurt, someone had jammed a copy of Edward Abbey's *Desert Solitaire* in my hand and demanded that I read it.

I am, I freely admit, a member of the cult of the word, and my gurus of the imagination awakened me to the simplicity of the natural world and the interdependence of all life. They taught me that a simple life was not only possible but one that could enrich and awaken you.

I lived the simplest of lives at the yurt, and one that brought me into intimate contact with the natural world. But while my literary heroes had given me a philosophical foundation, I had no experience with the practical and psychological aspects of living such an isolated existence. To compensate, I became a creature of habit. Many of my days were the same. I awoke at dawn, and the dog and I went outside. I usually tied her up in the early mornings, because that was when the rattlesnakes were most active. Then I'd stir the coals of last night's fire and get a pot of coffee going. The mysterious peaks of the Ortiz hid the dawn for a little bit, but the distant plains were everywhere washed in the golden desert sunlight. While it was still cool in the mornings, I worked on various activities. I built something for the yurt or went to get water or scratched at my worthless garden. When the sun started to heat things up, I went inside to write. I sat at my old Remington trying to hammer something together. Despite my hopes of being a writer, everything I composed while at the yurt was horrible. I kept at it because I needed the ritual in order to stay sane. In the hottest part of the day, the dog and I took a nap. The yurt had lots of open windows and was built in the shade of a large juniper. I slept on the built-in combination couch and bed with the dog curled in a ball at my side. Later, we'd wake and walk to the cow tank. We came back and I made dinner. I'd then sit and read in the coming darkness or watch the lights of Santa Fe come like stars into the night.

After I lived at the yurt for a while, the foreignness slowly began to vanish, and I became familiar with patterns and new ways of seeing. I began to learn the language of what I was seeing. I learned how the shape of the juniper and piñon trees echoed the shape of the yurt, or I delighted in the beauty of the desert's golden sunset. It may have been some romantic back-to-nature ideal that led me to the yurt, but what I found there was simply a new way of seeing. My everyday moment-to-moment life was not the projection of duty and appointment or the demanding modulations of some digitized screen but the exact importance of stone on stone, the precise shape of cliff, the intimate habits of coyote or deer, or the singular merits of this moment in time. Few among us can even repeat the color of today's sky or trace the shape of a horizon we've seen each day for years; but for that year I lived at the yurt, nothing in my life could have been more important.

Nearly forty years later I began to incorporate such lessons into the design for our Vermont house, working, as I said before, from the inside out. I learned, for example, how our bodies move differently depending on the task—ergonomics—and designed a kitchen accordingly, with different countertop heights so we could chop or mix or stir or nibble more comfortably.

I learned that plumbing is easier and more efficient if you cluster all the fixtures as close together as possible.

I learned I could use windows in interior walls to allow more light into an otherwise dark room.

I bought more rolls of freezer paper and used it to draw countless floor plans; I cut out scale-sized beds, chairs, tables, and toilets and arranged them on top of my floor plans to help me visualize things.

Slowly an idea of the outside of the house became clearer. For one thing, it would be a single-story house. Even though a two-story house is more efficient and simpler to heat, we wanted a house that would be easy to get around in as we grew older. It would also have lots of windows on the south side and not too many on the north. I considered such things as the location of doors and how much the roof should overhang, sunlight and privacy, solar gain and square footage.

I thought I had struck pay dirt when I came across an ingenious design for a house called the Eye. The oval eyelike shape is created by pulling two opposite corners of a square apart and then connecting the gaps with curved walls. Robert Andrews, who designs straw bale houses, realized that such a shape is very efficient when the corners are toward the east and west ends and the curved walls face south and north. This allows for great southern exposure, and the shape eliminates one of the main problems with building a round house: no straight walls. The Eye design has two traditional square rooms, yet a curved south-facing wall allows for maximum exposure to the winter sun.

Ultimately, I rejected the Eye for a variety of reasons. The foundation would be too complicated, and the roof design exceeded my abilities. However, Robert Andrews's Eye design opened a new way of thinking for me. I began to see a way to incorporate all our needs into a good but very simple home.

I designed a three-bedroom, 1,500-square-foot home. The house is a rectangle with the long sides facing north and south. It has a great room that serves as a kitchen, dining room, and entertaining area. There is a master bedroom and two smaller rooms—our office and den—which have fold-down couches to use for overnight company. One bathroom has a shower; the other has a built-in washer and dryer. The house has a small utility room and a storage attic that is accessible via a pull-down stepladder.

Our floor is made of concrete, stained and cut to look like Spanish tiles. We chose concrete (over my desire for a clay floor, which was roundly vetoed) because it would work best with our radiant floor heat and because it also absorbs the heat of the sun. The great room faces south and has four large picture windows. They provide an ever changing view of deep woods, distant hills, and sky. On sunny winter days, sunlight fills the entire room, heating it throughout the day.

It is human nature to bring familiar patterns of home and heart to a new place and to try to replicate them there, much as an infant might do in seeking the comfort of a familiar face in an unknown world. So it was, when I got to the basic rectangular design of our straw bale house—I realized that the deep-set doors and windows and the thick walls would look much like the small adobe houses I had come to love while living in the Southwest. I wanted to incorporate some of that beauty and simplicity into my design. I poured over books of historical photographs of buildings in Santa Fe and added elements like a certain window trim and wooden posts into my Vermont home.

That need for the familiar is also why we transplanted some of the plants from our Victorian house in town to the new land. We transplanted blueberry bushes and raspberries and moved some favorite flowers and bushes to our new house site.

I did the same thing long ago in New Mexico. I often borrowed a truck and used it to carry plants to the yurt. I dug up lilac bushes, iris, and wild holly bushes. A parent of one of my students gave me many of her flowers, and I roamed an arroyo digging up small cottonwood trees. Over the course of two months, I hauled several loads to the land and planted what I hoped would one day become a delightful garden.

We desire the comfort of familiar and simple patterns because they give us security in an otherwise foreign and ever-changing world. I hoped the flowers and trees would make the apparently barren desert look and feel like a home. In spite of my efforts, not a single plant survived, not even the cottonwoods; for although I planted them in an arroyo, it was much too dry there for them to grow. What I did not understand, and perhaps have not yet fully learned, was that happiness is found not in the things we try to carry with us but rather in acceptance of what is.

6

Foundations

"If you have built castles in the air, your work need not be lost; that is where they should be. Now put the foundations under them."

HENRY DAVID THOREAU, *Walden*

Before I left home, the foundation of my beliefs had been largely fashioned by my parents or my friends. I was lucky to have had a good education, and I knew my way around books and ideas. I liked the Beatles, loved Dylan. I had poured over the rich and fascinating pages of the *Last Whole Earth Catalog* and had read Thoreau's *Walden* more than once. I had smoked pot, done mushrooms, and hitchhiked my way all over the West. Still, I had not yet really ventured far from my 1950s midwestern Catholic ideals.

It was only after I left my Nebraska home and began teaching at Las Tres Villas school in Tesuque, New Mexico, that I began to trade my narrow and untested adolescent views for wider ones. Unlike the largely white town where I grew up, the majority of families in the three villages where I taught were Hispanic. Because of that experience, I had begun to understand and to joyfully accept the diversity of cultures in the world. In addition, the Vietnam War was raging; and with the possibility that I might be drafted any moment, I had an active personal interest in wanting to end the war. I was also spending more and more time at Cornucopia and other communes, and with that I began to learn more about how people might live and work together.

Because of all of this, I soon was swept up in the dream of living somewhere way out in the vast New Mexican landscape. When the people at Cornucopia told me they were going to build out near the ghost town of Madrid, I began to think about becoming their neighbor. All of us would live in our own places and come together whenever one of us needed help. Such dreams were in the air in those days, and it seemed as if youth, optimism, and, yes, even ignorance might change the world.

Two years before I built the yurt, counterculture hero Wavy Gravy created Earth People's Park in northern Vermont. He bought several hundred acres that he intended to be a mecca of self-sufficiency, a place with "free land for free people." Even the deed for the land was written so that it belonged to "all the peoples of the earth." People could visit or camp or build a shelter and live rent free for as long as they wanted. The idea was that people would come and create a place of harmony merely by virtue of wanting to live off the land.

Many people came, but few were prepared to survive the harsh Vermont winters. At its glory, there were probably twenty-five full-time residents, living in dispersed cabins, A-frames, canvas teepees, old school buses, geodesic domes, a 1950s vintage travel trailer, as well as an impressive eight-sided log cabin. Soon Earth People's Park attracted more than just these "hippie types." The prospect of free land brought gangs, drug dealers, outlaws, and destitute people in need of a home. The vision of "free land for free people" disappeared under the clouds of greed, selfishness, and poverty.

Still, I was a product of my era, and that culture—a counterculture at that—told me that getting back to the land was a cool way to live. Thousands and thousands of people tried it, but very few were successful. Most everyone failed: those in experiments like mine at the yurt or like Earth People's Park; those in communes, monasteries, or cults; and those simply in some drug-hazed rock 'n' roll dream.

The ones who survived refused to adhere to some idealized concept of heaven on earth. They were the ones who learned to live simply, prepared for whatever might come next, who held it as a commandment to do no harm in the world, who could cooperate with others, and who could silence the raging demands of their own desire.

In my case, the yurt was mainly a place where I could live so cheaply I wouldn't have to work. Oh sure, I had the general sentiment of the times, to "walk softly on Mother Earth"; but how to do that in a sustainable, practical way was beyond my youthful eyes. I was mainly looking for a place to live and, if necessary, to hide out in order to avoid being drafted into the war. I had built my castle of dreams high in the air. What I didn't understand was that my youthful foundation wasn't good enough to make those dreams last.

The entire plans for the yurt are printed on both sides of a single poster-sized sheet of pumpkin- orange paper. It was written in 1971 by a man from Maine, William S. Coperthwaite. A good part of one side of the sheet provides background information about the yurt. Coperthwaite explains that these structures have long been used by nomadic peoples in Asia. He also discusses the structure's aesthetic qualities. "Viewed from the outside the yurt is unimposing. With its low profile, sod covered roof, and wall of weathered pine it blends easily into the natural landscape." He goes on to explain that all the structural elements are functionally important and make the building stronger, less expensive, and simple. "The more simple a structure is, the more it is in harmony with the environment. In terms of design, simplicity gives a structure its beauty."

The plans for building the yurt start on one side of the sheet; and although they continue onto part of the other side, the entirety of the instructions, including the sod roof and the benches, is only twelve steps.

The directions for building the foundation of the yurt read as follows: "Make a 12' 8" diameter circle on the ground and divide it into 12 parts. At each of the 12 points on the circle, and at the center drive pipes into the ground level at the desired height. (The lower the Yurt can be, the more it will blend in with the landscape and the less imposing it will be.) An air space under the Yurt helps to keep it dry."

So it was that one hot morning in early May I stood on the desert with a pile of sharpened sticks at my side. I had picked a spot just a little way from the bank of an arroyo, with a good view of both the Ortiz and the distant shimmering mountains of Santa Fe. I began by driving the first stake into the ground to mark a center spot and tying a small rope to it. Before long I had marked the places where the footings would go. I had decided that instead of pipes, I would build the yurt on small pillars of stone. I began digging a shallow hole for my twelve foundation points.

I stopped a few hours later. I walked slowly up to the windmill. I was going to have a cool dip in the cow tank and then take a long siesta under a piñon tree. As I walked, the high-pitched drone of desert insects filled the air. When I reached the cow tank, I took a long cool drink from the pump. Amid the creaking of the windmill and the drone of the insects, there came another sound, a foreign, mechanical one. Someone had turned off the highway onto the desert and was driving toward the cow tank. I froze, not certain what to expect. In a moment, a jalopy of a rusted truck appeared, coughing blue-black smoke into the dusty air. It pulled up to me and stopped.

"Howdy," I said.

"Howdy." A young man, not much older than me, sat behind the wheel. He wore a beat-up soiled bandana and was shirtless.

I figured I needed to explain myself first. "I bought thirty acres down over there," I said. "I'm building a cabin there—well, a yurt anyway—for myself."

He smiled and nodded. "Then we're neighbors," he said. Neighbors? I had never seen anybody here before. He pointed, "My old lady and me have a place a few miles down the big wash." He said they were pretty self-sufficient and kept mostly to themselves. He was as surprised to see me as I was to see him. "It's getting pretty hot out there," he said. "Why don't you hop in? My old lady's got some food waiting."

A moment later we were bounding over an increasingly narrow set of ruts that led deep into the desert. A few miles later the ruts came to the lip of a valley and then sharply descended. In a small side canyon near the bottom, we came to a few cottonwoods growing in the shelter of a rock cliff. He turned toward them and stopped.

I looked around. Except for a crude wooden structure near the cliff face, an outhouse, and a few odds and ends scattered about, there was no way to tell that someone lived here.

I got out of the truck and followed him.

He was walking toward the wall along the cliff. A faded Mexican blanket hung over an opening. "I brought someone," he shouted out and then ducked through the opening.

I pushed back the blanket and stepped inside. It took a long moment for my eyes to adjust to the darkness. The wooden structure enclosed the entrance to a natural shelter in the rock face. The man stood near a wooden table. Near him was a dark-haired woman. "This guy's building a . . ." he turned to me. "What was that again?"

"A yurt."

". . . a yurt, off toward the highway. It's a long way away from here, way back up near the highway," he repeated, as if to reassure her. He motioned to me. "Come on and have a seat."

I made my way to the rear of the shelter. The table was a cast-off plank of wood that someone had put legs on. Behind the table, the cave narrowed considerably. The dirt floor rose up to a dark slit where there was a mattress, some milk crates of clothing and books, and a single kerosene lantern. I sat in one of the two mismatched chairs. The woman made her way between the table and a nearby metal food box. She was even younger than we were. She filled a plate with pinto beans and rice and handed it to me. While we ate, I tried to make small talk with her, but she didn't say much.

The man wasn't all that talkative himself. He said the cave made a great place to live. It was cool and comfortable and dry. He said that they got their water from a spring not too far away and that they cooked over an open fire down in the cottonwoods. Then he fell silent. The woman finished eating and crawled back to the mattress. There was just enough room for her to sit on it. She sat in the shadows, looking out at us.

The man told me that they were going to get a goat or a milk cow, but he needed to fence an area first. I offered to help him dig post holes.

"That would be far out," he said. "You serious?"

Before long we were outside digging holes in the rocky earth. It was still midday, but the deep cleft in the rimrock was already filling with cool shadows. Every once in a while we stopped working and followed a short path to a green oasis where water trickled from a crack in the rocks as if by magic. There were a few buckets and two or three ceramic coffee mugs that hung from a branch of a nearby piñon. We'd take a long slow drink, chat a little, and then head back to work. We cut poles from a cedar log, and by late afternoon we had set enough of them to fence off a grassy area near the spring. He offered me a ride back to the windmill, but I told him I was looking forward to the walk back. I turned to leave. The man gave me a handshake and said thanks. The woman hadn't come out of the shelter. I never saw either of them again.

When I finally settled on a design for our straw bale house, I turned my attention to the foundation. A foundation must be strong enough to support the weight of the building, high enough to keep the walls dry and off of the ground, and stable enough to have a level surface that won't shift when the ground freezes and thaws.

Finding an environmentally sound way to do this was not easy.

Foundations must be deeper than the frost line in order to prevent them from rising and falling with the cold. In Vermont that meant my foundation had to be at least four feet deep. In a house with a basement, the foundation also serves as the walls, but I was not going to have a basement. The traditional answer was to construct a four-foot-deep concrete frost wall for the house to sit on.

The mainstream way to make such a foundation is with poured concrete. As I said before, although it is handy, strong, and easy to use, concrete is not an environmentally wise choice. The trouble is finding a suitable alternative. The best alternative foundation I found was to use a design called a rubble trench. You dig a trench down to the frost line, put a drain at the bottom, and then fill the trench with gravel. Since the gravel and the drain prevent water from collecting, the foundation is not prone to freezing. You then pour an eight-inch concrete grade beam on top of the gravel and build your house on top of that. I liked the idea of using only eight inches of concrete rather than four feet.

But . . .

When I began the task of getting bids for the work, I talked to nearly every concrete contractor in the area. I showed them what I had in mind, but none of them had ever heard of a rubble trench.

Several old-timers reminded me this was Vermont, where we by god had real weather in winter and nothing but a deep solid wall of concrete could work. In the end, although rubble trenches have been successfully used in climates colder than Vermont, I could find no one who was willing to stake his reputation on helping me build one.

I gave up and chose to use a poured-concrete frost wall and turned my attention to how to insulate it. In order to further prevent frost heaves, the underground part of a foundation needs to be insulated. In mainstream construction, either foam is sprayed on or rigid boards made of something called extruded polystyrene are used. I didn't like the ecological consequences of using either of those products. Instead, I learned that boards made of spun mineral fibers—rock wool it is sometimes called—not only insulate well but also help to drain the foundation, since they are porous, like wool.

It looked as though I had found a perfect way to offset having to use so much concrete. Although I couldn't build a rubble trench, I wouldn't have to use synthetic insulation. Unfortunately, the mineral-wool boards were not easily available. A kindly older man who worked, of all places, at a nearby home-improvement big-box store eventually located a place in Canada that sold the boards. Rock wool wasn't a product the big-box store normally ordered, and that meant it would take two months or more for them to get it in. I didn't have that much time; so in the end, I had to abandon the idea of using rock wool and used the polystyrene boards. I chose them over sprayed-on foam because they insulate more evenly.

I finished installing the insulation on the foundation one evening in early June. That night, I slept at the land. I awoke before dawn, because my excavator Danny Thompson was due on-site by 6:30 a.m.

I had enough time before Danny arrived that the first rays of sunlight found me mowing the native grass I had planted over the septic system. I did not intend to have a lawn at my new house, but I knew that mowing the newly planted grass would allow it to make stronger roots and help to hold this newly disturbed earth in place.

I had just finished when Danny's truck bounced down the drive. He pulled up and stepped out of the cab. Danny is a man in his early forties. The first thing you notice about him is his size. He is a giant of a man, with an imposing frame, without an ounce of fat on it. Although his figure could make a grown man nervous, his face immediately puts you at ease. Handsome and rugged, he always has a twinkle in his eye.

After a few moments of conversation, Danny turned and hopped down into the trench next to the foundation. I jumped down beside him, and together we walked the perimeter of the wall, discussing what the busy day held.

"And the water line from the well?" Danny said. "Is that all set to be buried?"

"I think so," I said. "But maybe you'd better have a look-see."

At that, Danny jumped out of the trench to the ground. I followed suit, jumping up right behind him.

In the beginning, there was nothing but the pain. As I put weight on my right leg in order to hop up onto the ground, my knee simply stopped working. Instead of locking in place so that I could vault myself up, it buckled like a set of rain-soaked blueprints. I collapsed to the bottom of the trench. For that moment, my entire world shrank to the excruciating fire in my knee. I cried out, cradling my knee in my hands.

Poor Danny stood over me trembling. He could tell I was hurt and was not sure what to do. "Let me get you to the hospital," he stammered.

"No," I said. "Let me just see what's going on." Like a detached eyeball, I took stock of the situation. I lay in the dirt and contemplated what would happen if this meant I couldn't finish the house.

It may have been in the darkness of those thoughts that I found the courage to try to stand. I brushed away Danny's offer to help and sat up. It still hurt like the dickens, but I had to find out if I could put weight on my leg. I leaned on the frost wall and slowly stood up. My knee wobbled as if it might collapse again any second, and the pain was still intense. But I took a small step and another, and I discovered I could still move.

Danny hesitated. "Are you sure about this?" he said. "We could get you to the hospital and have somebody take a look at it."

It was not bravado that forced me to carefully climb out of the trench and begin timidly to move about but my fear that I wouldn't complete the house.

"Let's go," I said.

Won't I ever learn? Despite the differences in our ages, our conditions, and—for heaven's sake—our sizes, once I saw how easily Danny had leapt out of the trench, I naturally assumed I could do the same. My old familiar bugaboos of ignorance and pride had caught me once again.

It was a very tough day for me. I spent a lot of it finding jobs I could sit down to do. I never went to the hospital. As it turns out, I had sprained my meniscus, a pad of soft tissue in the knee that helps to reduce friction. A knee brace gave me enough stability to do most jobs that summer, but I always felt as if my knee might once again suddenly give out. I never felt secure on a ladder. And I started to ask my friends to handle any jobs that would have required me to be high in the air.

I did not know it when I lived at the yurt, but I was building a foundation for a lifetime of contemplation about simplicity and want, about selfishness and selflessness, and about how one's own choices ripple out to impact thousands of others beyond even the short span of a single life.

7

El Sol

I. Warmth

The man on the other end of the phone was emphatic. "Passive solar does not work well in Vermont," he repeated. I gulped. This was not just some yahoo who was speaking, but an authority. "There just isn't enough sunlight when you need it the most. Plus, you'll have a hard time keeping heat in with all those windows."

The man was a professor at a local college who specialized in alternative building methods. Despite a recent personal tragedy, he had generously agreed to speak with me on the phone about my plan to use sunlight to help heat our home.

I wasn't happy with what he was telling me. He must have felt my panic.

"Look, send me what plans you have, and I'll take a look at them," he said. "Then I'll tell you what I think of them."

"Are you sure?" I stammered.

"Send them," he said, and hung up.

My design called for three large south-facing windows that would allow the winter sunlight to help heat the interior of the house. With the concrete floor, I would have a good "heat sink," a way to store the warmth that the winter sun provides. At night the heat stored in the floor as well as in the straw bale walls would radiate into the house.

As much as possible, I was trying to design a passive solar house. "Passive solar" simply means orienting and designing a building to best capture and use the winter sunlight for warmth. The idea is an old one. The ancient people of the American Southwest built their stone and adobe buildings on south-facing cliff faces in order to use the natural heat of the sun for their homes in winter. In summer those same buildings would be shaded in the cool shadows of the cliff. And although the cave man and his old lady who lived near me at the yurt didn't have much, they *did* have a shelter that was easy to keep warm in winter and stayed cool in the summer.

During hot summer days, a properly oriented and designed modern passive solar house also stays cool and comfortable without air conditioning. My design called for wide eaves to shade the house in the summertime. The plan was that we would open all the windows on summer nights so that the floor absorbed the cool night air. In the morning, we would shut all the windows, and the thick straw would retain that coolness during the day.

But the professor had me worried. I knew that Vermont has the second-lowest maximum daily solar radiation per month of anywhere in the United States. The only place lower is the northern edge of Alaska. Still, there were several successful passive solar houses in Vermont, so I wasn't ready to give up on the idea.

Passive solar design is not only about designing heat sinks to store the sun's warmth; it can also include such things as solar slabs—concrete floors built on top of a system of vents that help radiate the warmth to all areas of the house by simply using heat's natural tendency to rise. I learned that it is critical to have the right combination of windows and floor mass; otherwise, passive solar will not work. Also, it is important to cover up the windows at night with shutters or insulated curtains in order to prevent the sun's warmth from escaping.

A couple of weeks later, the professor called me.

He thought we would realize only limited passive solar advantages, given Vermont's lack of winter sunlight, but made several recommendations to improve my design. For one thing, he suggested I reduce the number and size of the south-facing windows and increase the thickness of the floor. He told me I would need to cover the windows on winter nights to keep in the heat.

Finally, he said what I had been praying to hear: "If you do those things, I think this design will work in Vermont."

The first rule in building a passive solar home is to make sure it is properly oriented to the sun. You want the long side of your house facing the south so that on those cold but sunny winter days, your house absorbs the greatest sunlight. By the same token, in summer, when the sun is high overhead, such an orientation helps to shade the interior. In general you can be within ten degrees on either side of true south and still take advantage of this solar gain, but each location is a little bit different. I wanted to know *exactly* where the sun would be in midwinter at my house site so that I could orient the house in that precise direction.

The winter before we began building, I noted the position of the sun at the exact moment halfway between sunrise and sunset. At this solar noon, I took out my compass and recorded the sun's location low in the southern sky. Ideally, I wanted to know its position at noon on the solstice. But I knew I couldn't count on a sunny day in late December, much less at noon on the solstice, so every day it was sunny that winter I took a compass reading.

On the winter solstice I hit the jackpot. The day was clear, so I headed out to the house site. I was able to take an accurate compass reading exactly at midday. I felt pretty smug knowing how to position my new home to maximize free heat from the sun.

Several months later when it came time to dig the foundation, my excavator Danny started without me. Before I knew what was happening, he dug the first trench for the long side of the foundation. The amicable giant smiled down at me from the cab of the big machine. "Take out your compass," he said. "That trench I just dug will be facing due south." He grinned again and, as he closed the cab door, said, "You'll see. I'm good at guessing directions."

Sure enough, he was within a degree of due south. Still, he was three degrees off of my ideal winter solstice angle. I contemplated asking him to redo it, balancing my desire for perfection with the practical issues of time and money. As I watched Danny maneuver the big rig in order to dig the next trench, I decided to let it go—it was close enough.

Because of the passive solar orientation of our finished house, on many sunny winter days we use nothing but sunlight to heat the house. At night we fire up the woodstove for a few hours before bedtime. That heat combined with passive solar keeps the house at an average temperature of sixty-eight degrees.

To compliment this system and to serve as a backup, I installed radiant heat in the floor. Embedded in the floor is a system of plastic pipes that allows me to pump hot water through the floor in order to heat it. As it turns out, I seldom use the system, because our water is largely heated by propane and I'd just as soon conserve our use of the gas.

To limit our use of propane even further I installed a solar hot water system. An insulated pipe circulates nontoxic antifreeze through two solar panels mounted on my woodshed. In turn, the antifreeze heats the water going into my water heater, lowering the amount of propane we need.

While I was designing the house, I also learned it was possible to use the sun not only for electricity, passive solar heat, and hot water but also to heat *air* that then can be blown through the house with a fan. While solar electricity and solar hot water systems are not within the usual definition of "do it yourself," it is still possible to construct a homemade solar hot air device that is as efficient as a store-bought one and considerably cheaper.

Knowing that my airtight house would need an air exchange in order to circulate fresh air, I decided to incorporate a solar hot air system into it. I first installed a pair of insulated six-inch pipes that went from the cabinet where I would place the air exchanger, under the floor, and out through the foundation to where they popped up a few feet from the house. For a while, that's as far as this final experiment got. Once the house was finished and we moved in and regained our lives of jobs and socializing and living, the solar hot air box seemed quaint, belonging to an era when we were frenetic in our anxiety to make the house "work" right. Once we moved in and were able to heat the house easily using only passive solar heat and our woodstove, I put off building my experimental hot air box.

The two stubs that represented the unfinished experiment became the subject of animated conversations between my wife and me. Somehow she thought having two ugly pipes rising out of the strawberry patch right next to the house wasn't the most beautiful yard art. They didn't bother me because they were unsightly but because they represented unanswered questions: would such a system work, and could I become even less dependent on burning wood with the use of solar hot air? I finally convinced my lazy self to go ahead and build the darn thing. I figured that if it worked, great; and if it didn't, I would get rid of the marital annoyance by cutting down the unsightly stubs.

That is how I found myself one morning back at my familiar lumber store buying plywood, adhesive, screws, caulking, and more six-inch piping. "I thought you finished building your place," Ron said as he helped me load a couple of sheets of plywood onto the truck. I tried to explain about the hot air box. Ron grinned; he knew we had a house of straw (a "hay house," he often called it) and now figured I was back to my craziness.

What I wanted was to build a large wooden box with a piece of glass on one side. I would paint the inside of the box black and insulate the entire thing. Finally, I would connect the box to the two unsightly blue stubs in order to move the air in and out of the house. Just like the inside of a closed car on a sunny day, the air inside the box would heat up, and then the air exchange blower would push that hot air into the house.

On an unseasonably mild early November day, I set up my stained, chipped, cut, and bent sawhorses in the yard and went to work.

The first thing I realized was that a person forgets certain skills that have fallen into disuse. I didn't realize the plywood I had bought would make too flimsy a box until I had cut up the sheets. Another trip to town.

I spent the rest of that day fashioning an eight-by-four-foot box with thicker plywood. After that I turned my attention to how to insulate the thing. One of the strange consequences of building your own home is that you become a collector of leftover items. Find anyone who has spent time building, and you will have found someone who keeps such a collection. Hidden in various outbuildings around our place was my stash of odd pieces of lumber, concrete blocks, plumbing materials, nails, screws, clamps, and tools. Amid this clutter, I found a few odd pieces of extruded polystyrene (the solid pink sheets I used in order to insulate my foundation when I could not get the ecologically better mineral-wool boards).

I worked the better part of a day cutting the insulated boards to size and screwing them to the insides of my box. My evolving plan was to cover them with an insulated aluminum fabric and then paint them black so that the box would better absorb the sun's heat. At two o'clock in the afternoon, I stepped back to admire my work. I was figuring out just how I might support the glass window, when it dawned on me the mistake I had made.

Polystyrene is the same material that is used to make all sorts of things, from CD cases to plastic spoons and forks. Polystyrene water bottles as well as those forks and spoons are falling out of use, as people consider the carcinogenic properties of one of its main chemicals, styrene. When it gets hot enough, polystyrene is easily ignited. Burning polystyrene can release a cocktail of other unhealthy chemicals.

Had it been July rather than November when it dawned on me how stupid I was in planning to cover the *inside* of the hot box with pink board, my gapping mouth would have easily caught half a hundred flies.

Over the course of the next several days, I undid my work and then insulated the *outside* of the box. I also added four handles by extending two-by-fours beyond each corner.

Handles.

One thing I didn't mention was that Linda is of the opinion that my cool, space-age-looking big silver box covered in foil is *not* attractive and would be even *more* unsightly in our garden than the two plastic stubs in the strawberry patch. I'll never understand women; but to keep the peace, I agreed to make the thing portable so that it could be stored out of sight during the summer.

But now on bitterly cold but bright and sunny days in February and March, I throw a couple of louvers and divert the house's air exchange to a path that takes air outside where it passes through the solar hot air box. The air in the box can get quite warm. On a recent afternoon in late January the outside air temperature was

19 degrees, while the air inside the box was 170, a difference of 151 degrees. That day, the system raised the interior temperature of the house by 3 degrees.

The solar hot air box cost me $500.

II. Power

At night a single kerosene lantern lit up the yurt. On some nights, I simply crawled into my bed; but on other nights, I lit the lantern. After a moment, the glass chimney would begin to glow as bright as the noonday sun. I used that time to wash dishes, pouring hot water I had heated on the evening's campfire into a small plastic basin. Later I would set the lantern on my built-in desk and read or write letters. My typewriter ran on finger power alone. Once I snuffed out the lantern, the darkness was complete.

In the mornings, I sometimes used a small camping stove to heat water for coffee. The stove used canned heat, a jellylike substance made out of denatured alcohol. You opened a small can of the stuff and set a match to it. The stove itself was nothing more than a metal frame that held the can and provided a surface large enough to hold a small cooking pot. My supply of the cans was low, so I cooked on the open fire and only used the small stove for the immediacy of coffee in the mornings. On cold nights in winter, I lit the woodstove for warmth and used the top to cook.

Firewood was never a problem. The desert piñon tree consists of as many dead branches as green, and my plateau was speckled with an endless supply of them. I cut branches off with a handsaw and dragged them back to the yurt.

I didn't have a television, of course, or a radio. I had a small, battery-powered cassette tape player and a handful of cassettes for entertainment. When that failed, I took out my old guitar and strummed tunes for the dog. A deck of cards allowed me the schizophrenic pleasure of a night of solitaire.

Not so, these modern times. In our old Victorian house in Vermont, Linda and I had a television, computers, hair dryers, microwaves, a toaster oven, stereo, cordless phones, electric coffee grinders, and a myriad of other modern conveniences. We knew our electricity would not come cheaply at our new house site. That was our fault, since we chose the more remote "artist's" site on which to build our house. Because of the site's remoteness, bringing power to it would be expensive. The electric company's cost estimate for stringing power to the place was almost as expensive as installing an off-grid solar-powered electricity system. However, the decision to install a solar photovoltaic system had had less to do with economics and more to do with an event from my childhood.

One day in the late 1950s, I was sitting at the counter of Wagey's Drugstore, just down the street from my home. I was sipping a green river and flipping through the most recent issue of *Popular Mechanics*. Suddenly I felt as if I had been transported to some fantasy of the future. In the magazine, I read that scientists had invented something called a solar cell, which converted the sun's energy directly and efficiently into electricity. I was spellbound as I flipped through the pages of drawings, pictures, and words explaining how the device worked. The cells were a tiny semiconductor sandwich made with a thin layer of silicon. One side was covered with boron, and the other with phosphorus. One side produced a surplus of electrons, the other a deficit. Photons from sunlight hit the wafer and knocked off some of the electrons on one side of the cell. Electricity was created as surplus electrons from one side tried to migrate to the other. While a single cell did not produce much electricity, I learned you can put a lot of them on a single panel so that the power adds up in a hurry. There were no moving parts.

For the next few months, before something else consumed my childhood imagination, I could think of nothing more than these tiny mysterious miracles. A half century later, that memory still lingered so much that it no doubt played a part in our decision about electricity.

One possibility we explored was to have *both* a photovoltaic system *and* an on-grid electrical tie-in. In the dark months of winter, we would buy most of our power from the electrical company; but in the sunnier months, we could sell power generated by the solar panels back to the company. This grid-tied system allows the homeowner to net-meter—that is, to have your electric meter run backward when you are generating electricity from the sun. Because there is no need to store power on-site in batteries (as there is with our off-grid home), the system is cheaper than having solar power alone. Also, you can feel pretty good about the fact that you are helping to supply power for your friends and neighbors.

For us, however, the cost of both bringing in power and installing a photovoltaic system was prohibitive. We had to either buy power or find a way to be independent of the power grid.

We looked into other sources. It would be possible to install a small hydroelectric generator at the brook, but we decided it wouldn't work. The amount of electricity decreases the farther it has to travel along a wire, and the house site was too far from the stream. We wouldn't get enough power to make it cost-effective. Likewise, a home-sized wind tower wouldn't work well because our land is largely sheltered from the wind.

We filled out a solar worksheet, listing the appliances we use, in order to calculate how much electricity we thought we needed. Armed with the results, we began to collect bids from some local companies that install photovoltaic systems. The cost of even the cheapest was beyond our budget. Back to the worksheet. We would need to cut our consumption, but how? In most homes, the refrigerator uses the most electricity. We were told about a super-efficient model that used four to five times less electricity, but its

$3,000 price was prohibitive. With a bit of searching, we discovered a small, reasonably priced Frigidaire that used only a little more electricity than the expensive refrigerator. To further reduce our consumption, we would stop using a cordless phone and would buy the most efficient washer and dryer.

With a more modest use of electricity and careful selection of efficient appliances, we were able to get a bid for a smaller photovoltaic system. It was still expensive, but it was now affordable.

Our decision to install an off-grid solar electrical system meant some changes in our life style but not an inconvenience. Now we check the weather forecast before we do laundry. We wait until a sunny day, when we have a surplus of electricity, before we do the wash. We chose a propane water heater over an electric one. We found a pump for our water well that was designed to work with a small off-grid system like ours. At night we use our laptop computers' batteries, and recharge them during the day. Other electronic devices such as televisions, entertainment systems, and radios are *always* using electricity. Even when you turn them off, they keep using electricity, called a "phantom load," so that they will come on instantly when you press Power. I installed wall switches and connected them to the outlets where we plug in our television and stereo system. Now we simply flick a light switch to turn them on and flick it off when we are finished. This simple addition further reduced our power consumption. Likewise, an off-grid system requires some regular home maintenance. From time to time you have to check the water level in the bank of batteries, where the sun's power is stored, and a few times a year you have to tilt the angle of the panels to better face the sun. Also, even after it is installed, an off-grid system still costs you some money. The batteries need to be replaced around every seven to ten years, for example.

Still, these are minor shifts in our life, and they have made us more aware of the ever-changing sky and weather and something as beautiful, simple, and profound as the rising and setting of the sun.

III. El Sol

Most nights on the desert, I slept inside the yurt. But on other nights, even some milder winter nights, I'd haul my sleeping bag outside and sleep under the stars, waking early to watch a pink line of dawn come toward me from the east. Ho hum, I'd laugh, stretching and yawning at the brilliant sun cutting the lip of the distant horizon, another sunny day. I relished those bright sunny days. The spirit of the sunlight itself was all I needed of religion or philosophy or of life itself.

That was probably a good thing, because the yurt itself was not well built for either the heat of the sun or the deep cold of winter. While I put insulation in the floor, the walls of my yurt had very little, and I never insulated the roof at all. The building plans called for a sod roof. With the bucolic voice of the era, they read, "The sod should be put down in two layers, the first with the grass side down and the second with the grass side up. The second layer should overlap the joints of the first to hold the sod in place until it can grow together. The roof will need watering until the grass grows long enough to shade itself. The longer the grass, the cooler the inside in the summer. Plant flowers on your roof."

I did none of that. I knew it would be impossible for me to establish and maintain a sod roof in the dry, sun-drenched New Mexico desert. Instead, I spent many days sealing my roof with a nasty tar-like compound and covering the entire thing with tar paper in order to keep out the rain and snow.

While the insides got pretty warm on the hottest summer days, I built the yurt under the cool shade of a couple of large juniper trees that helped make it tolerable during the warmest hours of the day. Likewise, with so little insulation, my little home gave up heat easily in winter. Luckily, I had borrowed a great wood-stove from a friend, for I wouldn't have been able to afford to buy one. That stove was able to keep the interior warm all night with just a small fire.

As I said earlier, to prevent periods of insanity, I often ritualized my days: coffee at my fire pit in the dawn's early light, work on the yurt's roof or other projects in the cool mornings, and a book and an afternoon nap or a walk to the windmill for water during the heat of the day. Sunset came with my meager meal boiling over the evening's campfire.

On other days, however, I purposely broke the ritual or had it broken by circumstances.

One morning, while still seated outside sipping my coffee, I heard my dog barking somewhere on the desert. I realized suddenly that I'd been hearing her for some time. I threw my cup down and started running, shouting her name. She wasn't too far away. Just before I reached her, I heard the dry hiss of the rattles.

The dog pranced in front of a small cluster of pin cushion cacti. Less than two feet away was a western diamondback, its head raised above a coiled and undulating body. Seeing the snake's open mouth and my dog's incessant barking made it appear for an instant that, instead of deadly combat, the two of them were simply speaking to one another.

The rattles hissed without end.

Before I finally reached her, she responded to my command and came to me. I grabbed her collar, and as I began to scold her for not coming, I noticed tiny pinpricks of blood on one of her legs. She was a small dog, less than thirty pounds; the poison would kill her quickly.

I took her in my arms, calming her and stroking her head. I carried her back to the yurt and went inside. I don't remember when I started to cry, but I set her down and sat on the floor beside her, speaking softly to her.

After a moment, she curled up at my side. Outside, the heat of the sun was growing. She fell asleep; and I waited for death. I decided I would bury her at a nice overlook not far from the yurt. I would cover the spot with stones to keep out the coyotes. I found comfort in the thought that she would be returning to the dust of that magnificent desert plateau. She had been a fine dog and my constant companion for years.

But she did not die, not until years later. In a little while, she stood up, eager to resume her morning romp around the desert. I kept her tied the rest of the day so that I could watch her. Either the snake's fangs had passed through the loose skin of her leg, or the wound was from a cactus.

When I believed she was dying, I thought of many things. I contemplated how all life is impermanent, how the juniper trees, the rattlesnake, the dust of the desert, and even the very sun itself would pass away. Death itself is a part of the interdependence of all things. We are so lightly here, under this bright and life-giving sun.

8

Economics

For Trish—in celebration of her first year of teaching

When, in 1988, the exiled Vietnamese monk Thich Nhat Hanh called for a "deep ecology," he was echoing a growing scientific understanding that human life is dependent on a harmonious balance of interdependent relationships between organisms. In order to maintain this balance, we humans must learn to act in a much more mindful way, aware of the implications of *all* our actions. It isn't enough to want to protect the earth—we need to go deeper and confront the pollution in our own consciousness. There is little difference between the violence we do to the land and the violence we do to one another. "If we change our daily lives—the way we speak, think and act—we change the world," he wrote. "The best way to take care of the environment is to take care of the environmentalist."

During the time I was preparing to build the yurt, I had a crisis that made me confront the implications of my own actions. It came in the form of a letter I received a few months before I built the yurt. It was an official response to my request to be exempted from military duty. I had applied for status as a conscientious objector, a classification that allowed you to avoid service as a military combatant based on religious, moral, and ethical beliefs. While I had never thought too deeply about the ethical, much less

Fig. 3. First day of classes at Tesuque School
(photo courtesy *The New Mexican*)

the environmental, implications of violence, I was certain that killing was morally wrong.

The letter informed me that my request for a CO status had been denied. Instead, I was being classified 1-A: fit for military service. It meant that I could be drafted any day to serve in Vietnam.

The day after I received the letter, I stood in front of my fifth-grade students at the Tesuque school, in a dark and somber mood.

We were seated outside on the lawn of the old village church, which served as the schoolhouse.

"I have a difficult question to ask you," I announced to my fifth graders. "Who here believes that they would never kill another human being?" Most of the hands shot up. "Wait," I said, "let me finish." We had just completed a unit about Hitler and World War Two. I asked them to consider how we could ever stop such madmen. Most of the hands went down. What if someone threatened to kill your mom or dad? Only three hands remained in the air.

"Benjie, would you please come up here?"

He got up from the class circle and stood in front of me. Benjie was very small for his age, but he was well liked and intelligent. I picked him because I knew he was one of the most peaceful kids at the school. I knew he used his intellect, humor, and common sense to solve the myriad of conflicts that are a part of being a ten-year-old boy on a boisterous schoolyard.

I repeated the fundamental question. "You would *never* kill anyone?" The rest of the students grew quiet.

"No, never."

"Why?"

Benjie paused and then spoke with confidence. "It is not a good thing," he said. "Only bad things can come from killing. If people no longer killed each other, people could work together to make things better."

I reached into my pocket and took out a pocket knife. I unfolded the largest blade. I bent to the ground and slammed the point into the dirt. "At the count of three I am going to go for that knife, and then I am going to kill you."

The class roared with laughter.

I know what you are thinking. In today's world my actions would likely land me in jail. At the very least, I could expect to be fired. But the Tesuque school was being built on trust. The parents trusted and respected us as teachers. We were all in this thing together: trying to save the community school. It was uncommon ground, and yet everyone understood and believed in the effort. The parents gave the teachers full freedom (what clse could there be, given the unique way the school had come into being?) to experiment in our classrooms.

I waited until the laughter died down. Benjie was grinning ear to ear.

I had not changed expression. "At the count of three," I repeated, "I am going for that knife."

Benjie's grin disappeared. The class was dead silent. I began to count.

"One, two . . ."

Benjie leapt for the knife. He grabbed it and threw it across the lawn. The class cheered.

When I came back with the knife, Benjie had sat back down.

"We're not through," I said.

He stood.

I put the knife back in the ground. "One," I began, "two . . . three!"

He looked at me an instant and then turned and ran. I grabbed the knife and took off after him. Someone in the class screamed; the rest began to cheer.

Benjie ran, circling the church.

We raced past the third-grade class. They stopped and stared. We ran past the principal's trailer. The principal, Mollie, was just stepping outside with a reporter from the Associated Press. The two of them stood with their mouths open, watching that tiny student running for his life, chased by a bearded wild hippie carrying a knife.

When we rounded the final side of the church, I was fearful my unattended class had simply scattered into the field we used as a playground. Instead, they were all on their feet, cheering for Benjie.

I let Benjie beat me back. When he reached the class, he stopped and pumped his arms into the air for effect. Just then I reached him. I lifted him up. He was so small I could do so with ease. "Are you all right?" I whispered. He grinned and nodded. "Okay, play along with this." With dramatic flair, he let me pin him to the ground. I raised the knife high above my head and, for effect, stabbed it into the dirt at his side.

I stood and gave a growling cheer and beat my chest. Benjie sprang up and stood next to me. Everyone was talking at once. For the rest of the period, I led the class in a far-ranging discussion of morals and ideas and the nature of power.

It was a bit selfish of me, I'll admit, but teaching that class gave me a lot to think about. The next day, I wrote a letter to my draft board in Nebraska, appealing my classification as fit for military service.

A while later they replied and told me they would grant me a "courtesy hearing."

I went into panic mode. If the board did not accept my written request, how could I ever convince them simply by talking to them? I got ahold of a copy of Alan Blackman's booklet *Face to Face with Your Draft Board*, which sold over thirty thousand copies in the first ten months, and read it a dozen times on my flight back to Lincoln. The booklet was full of useful information, but it did not make me hopeful about my chances: "As volunteers who help the Selective Service System, it is likely that board members will be biased against CO."

I arrived early, but they were already waiting for me. I was led into a poorly lit conference room, where several men sat around a long table. The only open seat was at the end of it. All the men were white, save one black man who sat directly to my right. They all wore suits.

I was allowed to begin. I tried to explain my moral objections to violence.

In high school I was introduced to the great authors of peace by my teachers. I read Thoreau and Gandhi, Dorothy Day and St. Francis. I studied the Quakers and the Buddhists. What they all said seemed to be so simple: you pledged not to resort to violence or physical force in defiance of anything. I believed Gandhi's words when he said that war leads only to dictatorship and that only nonviolence leads to peace.

I tried to explain all of this to those stern men seated in that dark room. When I fell silent, they began to ask me about my job at Tesuque School. I tried to tell them that I *was* serving the country in my job at Tesuque. I explained how the three Hispanic villages came together to create their own school, etc., etc. The more I spoke, the more I came to realize that the story of the school only reinforced their opinion I was some kind of long-haired hippie freak.

The man seated to my right spoke for the first and only time. "You are doing all this work for only five dollars a *day*?"

I shrugged. I explained I was living with a family. They helped with room and board.

He looked me squarely in the eye. "I can't believe you are surviving on just five dollars a day," he said.

I left that room feeling like a condemned man. I realized that soon I would have to either hide out or head to Canada. "Some of the Draft Board's emotional behavior," the booklet had warned me, "may stem from an ignorant super-patriotism, from their own compromises, their own experiences in the army, or from their own fears about violence." I got back to New Mexico and warned my colleagues at school that I could be quitting any day. I contacted an old friend who had moved to Canada to avoid being drafted and let him know I might be headed north. I studied the plans for the yurt and decided, if nothing else, I would hide out on the desert until I figured out what to do next.

Instead, I was classified as a conscientious objector.

To this day, I believe that the sole reason I obtained a CO was that man's concern about the *economics* of my life. I was making $100 a month, far below the poverty level. Somehow that information must have swayed his opinion. Apparently he equated my volunteer poverty with military service in Vietnam.

Getting such a CO was unusual in those days, and I took a foolish pride in thinking of myself as a peaceful man. But the truth was that just as my friends who were headed to Vietnam had no real understanding of war, I had no real understanding of peace. The only thing I had learned from my childhood was that my imagination was horribly inadequate when it came to the real possibilities for catastrophe in the world.

Like any twentieth-century American kid, I grew up in the shadows of violence.

My parents were both veterans of World War Two. While my mother told us chilling stories of the soldiers who filled the hospital beds where she served as a nurse, my father never talked about his experiences. When pressed, my mother would give us only vague details about his time during the war. "Your dad saw some awful things," she would say somberly. "He has a right not to talk about it."

My father continued to serve in the Army Reserves for the rest of his life. Once or twice a year he would leave for an extended stay at an Army Reserve camp. And every week, on Monday nights, he put on his starched uniform and drove to the far side of town to meet with other reserves.

It was also on Monday evenings that my town tested the air-raid sirens that would one day tell us that nuclear bombs were coming. At 5:00 p.m. sharp, a screaming came across the sky as dozens of sirens—perched on office buildings and schoolhouses all over the city—came to life. The cold, sudden wailing rose steadily until it seemed as though the very birds would never again be heard.

The real violence, of course, was also much closer to home.

One day in 1958 a redheaded nineteen-year-old punk from my hometown, named Charlie Starkweather, pulled up to his girlfriend's house, walked inside, and, at point-blank range, shot her parents and her sister to death. Then Starkweather and his girlfriend hopped into his car. Together they roamed the city for five days while Starkweather killed nearly everyone they met. He killed a young man who had helped them when their car wouldn't start. He killed another two men who had helped them when they got stuck in a snow bank. He killed a housewife and then shot her dog. Before they were captured, eleven had died. Like other families, we stayed locked up tight in our home, afraid to answer even a knock on the door.

Fistfights were a regular feature in the park next to my junior high school. I had a cowardly streak, and so I tried to avoid them. But every once in a while, when push came to shove—as it often did in my adolescent years—I pushed back. Then the tight circle of boys pressed close around; and like dancers, we began to pound at each other, bare fist on head and chest, until finally, in a whirlwind of curses and threats, it ended. I would walk home alone in the darkening sky, shaking and trembling, the blood still drying on my fists.

However much we abhor the violence around us, we must also be constantly aware that we too are capable of brutal, unspeakable acts of hatred. Fear and anger smolder just below the surface of our everyday world. How *do* those flames first ignite? How can I ever put such a fire out?

This "deep ecology" is not for the cowardly. Peacefulness has to be relentlessly pursued in the face of the raging violence all around us. Peacefulness presupposes both the ability and the courage to strike; but it demands our conscious restraint to calm our own desire for vengeance. To know true peace, I have to be mindful each and every moment, and I must first look deep within myself.

Gandhi insisted that we could not look at the butchery going on in the world with indifference. "I have unchangeable faith that it is beneath the dignity of man to resort to mutual slaughter," he wrote. "I have no doubt that there is a way out."

9

The Beautiful Tree and Other Disasters

It was what I call a great-grandmother tree, a sugar maple of such incredible girth and height that it dwarfed all else, an ancient giant whose towering branches and centuries of seeds had propagated generations of offspring. There are perhaps a dozen such trees on the ten acres of our Vermont property, but this one might have been the oldest and the largest of them all. The massive trunk rose from a soft bed of ferns and wild strawberries then widened slightly, the result of some long-ago obstruction in its growth. The size of the trunk did not seem to diminish even as it climbed higher and higher. The giant rose nearly eighty feet into the air before the first lateral branches, themselves the size of trees, arched from the trunk. At its crown, far above, branches opened to the sky in twisted, muscled arms.

The canopy was massive and so high above the other trees that it shaded much of the surrounding woods. In summer screeching blue jays hid high inside the green tangle, while in fall wild turkeys spent the night huddled together on its barren gray branches.

From the start, I knew I wanted to save that tree. I built the driveway around it so that people who came to our door could park in the shade of its beauty. On the days we poured the foundation and floor, the burley big men who drove the concrete trucks had to navigate around it, the huge trucks twisting and turning to avoid a collision.

One early morning in June, I was walking down the driveway, when I realized the beautiful tree would have to go. I stood and stared. What a dumbbell I'd been. Up until that time, the house had been nothing more than a concrete slab; but the previous week, we had started to build the wooden post-and-beam frame for the house. About half the slab was encircled by the frame, enough so that I could get an idea of what it might look like to have the entire house sitting just there.

That's when it struck me. While the ancient maple tree was a good forty feet from the house, its immense size meant that if it fell, it would not only hit the house but could crush it. I looked back and forth a dozen times; and each time, I knew there was no choice but to cut the tree down.

It wasn't going to be easy. There was only one place the big maple could fall without getting hung up in the surrounding trees: a narrow open space the well digging crew had cleared to set up their rig.

I was not confident enough with a chain saw to cut down such a massive tree, much less to set it down exactly where it needed to go; so I called my friend Jon Fitch.

Jon is a thin older man with a striking wispy white beard. Although he has a slight frame, he is stronger and has more energy than many men half his age. Despite the handicap of being a professor of psychology, Jon has a lot of experience when it comes to chain saws.

He showed up early that afternoon.

"You weren't kidding," he said, hopping out of his truck. "That's quite a maple." He walked over to it and then began circling it, stomping down the surrounding brush to make it easier for us to work near it.

Even when standing still, Jon is never standing still. Today he was on full charge. Soon we were both caught up in the task before us. We made preparations for the big event, such as clearing things out of the way so we could run quickly if something went wrong. As we worked, we talked through what was going to happen, where I would be standing, which way Jon should run when the tree started to topple, and the best way to get it to land exactly where we wanted it to. We studied the tree closely, as if we could discern its desires in this mess.

Linda stood at the top of the drive, nervously watching us prepare.

Finally we were ready.

Felling a tree is done using three cuts. You start on the side where you want it to fall and use two cuts to remove a wedge. The wedge needs to be just the right depth and angle in order for the tree to fall correctly. Given how exact we needed to be with the big tree, we spent considerable time figuring out just where to cut the wedge. We measured and even drew precise lines on the trunk with a marker to guide us.

I moved Jon's truck while he made sure his chainsaw was ready. Of his three chainsaws, the one he chose to use on the maple was the largest. The extra-long bar—the business end of a chainsaw—was designed for cutting down the largest trees.

When everything was in place, Jon looked at me and then pulled on the starter rope. He pulled again and once again. The chainsaw coughed and then roared to life. At close range, the whine of a chainsaw can be deafening. Jon wore ear protection; I did not.

He knelt at his saw, adjusting the speed. He stood, hoisted the saw, and began.

His wedge cuts were beautiful—smooth as glass and perfectly in line with the marks we had drawn. After several moments of the buzzing saw, blue smoke, and flying wood chips, he turned off the saw. With a small sledgehammer, Jon knocked the large wedge of wood out of the trunk. It fell to the ground, exposing the perfect cut he had made. He looked at me again.

I nodded and headed for the hills, still hobbling with my injured knee.

The third and final cut is made on the side opposite the wedge. It must be perfectly horizontal and slightly higher than the bottom of the wedge in order for the tree to fall correctly.

Jon held the roaring chainsaw carefully against the trunk. He looked high into the tree and then behind him, reviewing one last time his escape route in case anything went wrong. He began.

Though the tree was enormous, I knew his chain was sharp and he'd cut through it quickly.

Then he yelled something above the roar of the saw. The tone of his voice, more than the words, made me take immediate notice. "It's falling the wrong way!"

Linda, who witnessed the entire event from the top of the drive, told us later that I shouted "Run!"

Jon turned off the saw and scrambled up the driveway to where I stood. "It moved a tiny bit," Jon was breathless from sheer adrenalin, "but it moved the wrong way: it pinched my saw." The tree still stood, but the chain saw was stuck in the trunk of the massive tree like a mosquito under the toe of an elephant.

There ensued forty-five full minutes of absolute, ice-cold, bloody panic.

We had to find a way for the tree not to fall on the concrete slab.

At first we thought we might be able to somehow sling a rope around the maple, hitch it to the pickup truck, and pull it over. We abandoned that idea a minute later when we realized there was no way we could get the rope high enough to do any good.

Linda rounded up two gas company men who had been working at our neighbors' house. The men looked at the tree and said we had a problem.

"If we had an excavator with a bucket on the front," Jon said, "we could maybe push it over."

"Maybe," the men said, and then just shook their heads. They climbed back in their truck and drove away.

"There're a couple of men who have excavators not far from here," I offered.

Jon stood in a kind of trance, staring at the tree.

I turned to Linda. "Jon and I will go try to find someone to help," I said. "You stay here in the drive to make sure that if anyone comes, they don't go anywhere near that tree." I walked toward the truck. "Jon?"

He turned away from the tree so slowly I thought he barely moved. He shuffled his way to the truck in a kind of zombie stupor.

"You all right?" I asked when he got in.

"Let's go," he said.

I sped out of the drive and over the hill where I knew two contractors lived. I didn't hold out much hope, however. It was midweek on a glorious June day during what was to be the last summer of the big housing boom. Anyone who owned an excavator was long gone and working somewhere. Sure enough, there was no one around at the first house. At the second, the man's wife said that he was completely booked but might be able to help us sometime next week.

"Thanks," I said to her, "but this is kind of an emergency." I turned the truck around and headed down the driveway. "I'm going to try one more place," I said. "There's a logger down the road who might be able to help."

One of the oddest things about building my own house was how it affected my way of thinking. I developed a strange ability to doggedly forge ahead while shrugging off any emotional attachment to the consequences. Currently the issue was the tree. I was calculating how many days I would be set back if the tree smashed the frame, or worse, cracked the foundation. I was neither happy nor unhappy but driven like some emotionless robot. Building my own house was a monumental undertaking, and I knew that if I allowed myself to panic . . . Well, let's just say that I tried not to think about how it made me feel inside; for if I did, I would never have the courage to finish the house.

The early afternoon sky was clear blue. The June sunshine was warm.

The logger was in his log yard, unloading tree-length logs from a semi; a one-man operation, he didn't have a moment free to help us.

As I turned around in the logger's yard, Jon spoke for the first time since we left my house site. "Drive into town. There has to be someone we can find."

"No," I said. "I'm going back. I'm going to block the driveway so that no one can drive in. Then Linda and I will go home and try calling places on the phone."

Suddenly Jon became animated. "I was overly confident. But the wedge was perfect. I don't know what went wrong. I should have stuck a plastic prying wedge into the tree trunk when I first started cutting . . ."

He was frantic; his voice grew in pitch. "The entire tree shifted the wrong direction; it was just a fraction of an inch. It shouldn't have, but it did. "He began to sway and bounce in his seat. His moan caught me off guard. "I am paying for whatever damage this causes."

"Don't be silly," I said.

He was crying. "I am going to pay for the damage," he sobbed. "I'm so sorry . . ."

In the twenty-five years I had known him, I had never seen Jon cry.

Fig. 4. Cutting up the tree after it fell

"Jon, listen; it's all right," I said. It was that emotionless ro-bot speaking, something disemboweled from human feelings, set only on a task that needed doing. I said my goal was simply to take down the tree and make sure no one got hurt. I told him I knew before we started that it might not fall right. I knew it might hit the house but figured it was better to hit the house now than a year from now. The slab and house were really not important, and I told him so. But he didn't even hear me much less believe me.

Linda was standing blocking the entrance to our road. She stood with one thumb up and one thumb down. She had been pacing at the road when she heard a distant, deep thud and knew it had fall-en. Thumbs up: it didn't take down our framing. Thumbs down: it had hit the slab.

She climbed in the truck with us, and I drove down the drive. When I reached the hill above the house, I stopped the truck. The space where the beautiful tree once filled the air was now vacant sky, and the orderly symmetry of the rectangle that was to be our home was now filled by the massive gray bulk of the felled tree.

The maple had fallen exactly 180 (not 179, not 181) degrees from where we'd planned.

What we had not known, and had not prepared for, was that the interior of the beautiful tree was rotted. Instead of being solid, the core of the tree was nothing more than soft wood, wet and crumbling to a dark, putrid brown. Because of that, it had fallen the wrong way, across the entire northeast corner of the slab. The upper branches of the crown spread over half of the floor—the thick green foliage, like some grotesque household furniture.

Jon and I spent the next several hours cutting up the tree and hauling branches away. We worked like men possessed—each of us manic with self-recrimination, doubt, and guilt.

I had just started living at the yurt when the disastrous fire at the Cornucopia commune destroyed the A-frame. The son of one of the couples was supposed to tend the woodstove in the A-frame, but something happened and the place caught on fire. By the time the local volunteer fire department arrived, all they could do was watch and make sure the fire didn't spread to other buildings.

Aside from the A-frame, Cornucopia consisted of an old adobe house, a couple of sheds that had been converted into small independent dwellings, and an assortment of outbuildings.

Cornucopia began life as a small collection of couples who had a common desire to live in a cooperative manner. Since hordes of people were flocking to the desert Southwest, jobs were hard to come by. No one had much money. My friends from long ago had shared what they had and tried to live a deliberate life. The couple who owned the property, Jim and Margaret, were the parents of two children: a girl about eight and an older boy, the one whose accident caused the fire. Jim was very handy with tools and a resourceful man. Margaret was hardworking too, and she had a clever wit that often came to the rescue in conflicts.

The second couple, Randy and Mary, were recent immigrants from the East Coast. They were crafts people who made stained glass objects like lampshades and window frames, and they made a little money selling stuff to tourist shops in Santa Fe. They were Quakers and lovingly called one another "thee" and "thou."

Bob—my friend who helped me build the yurt—and his wife, Laura, had just moved onto the commune with their infant son. Bob had quit a job as a high school drama teacher on the East Coast and had just moved to New Mexico. He had decided to quit teaching and hoped to start a life in New Mexico as a carpenter. He had learned the trade from his father back East but had not yet found a paying job out West. He made what little money he could by doing small repair jobs.

Added to this assortment were occasional people like me—hangers-on who always managed to show up often enough to help with chores in exchange for a good dinner, plenty of wine, and always interesting conversations.

Cornucopia's residents were united by a simple desire to live together cheaply and harmoniously. They made it a ritual to share the evening meal as a group; that way, they could discuss any problems that needed to be talked about. The idea was to share work and responsibilities equally, and they also enjoyed one another's company.

The commune movement was probably at its peak in 1972, and New Mexico was at the epicenter. It's easy to imagine from this distance—with history fading into small, bite-sized chunks—that a hippie commune was full of tie-dyed, pot-smoking, free-love, long-haired, unwashed weirdoes who did no work and never bathed. The truth was that Cornucopia, like most communes, was an attempt to find a more sustainable way of living. If ten or twenty or even hundreds of people could figure out how to live together united by a common belief that they could create a more peaceful, cheaper, healthier, and even easier life, then such a change might ultimately influence the world for the better. While such idealism spawned everything from Earth People's Park to the death cult at Jonestown, most of the communes back then were simply groups of people trying to make things better for themselves and find a way to live life without harming others.

The fire was the beginning of the end of Cornucopia. I never knew much about the details, but fingers pointed and relationships soured. Soon everyone simply went their separate ways.

What the disaster at Cornucopia meant to me was that my isolation at the yurt would be complete. Prior to the fire, the commune had planned to relocate on eighty acres of land almost adjacent to mine. I had counted on having (and tried to reassure my rightfully worried-to-death mother that I would have) the commune as my neighbors. Instead of having a community, I now had to confront the fact that I would be living in total isolation on that high lonely plateau.

10

- - - - - - - - - -

The Amoeba

Miraculously the maple tree missed the finished framing of the straw bale house by mere inches. The damage to the slab was minimal, especially considering the power to which it had been subjected. The next day, my neighbor came to remove the largest chunks of the massive tree with his tractor; he estimated that it had weighed nearly eight tons. The bulk of it had hit the sill plate I had installed just that morning. The pressure-treated two-by-six wooden plank looked like a slab of squished butter. Panicky, I replaced it quickly and hurried to finish framing the house in order to be ready in time for the biggest deadline of the summer: installing the roof trusses.

Jon, he of the disaster with the beautiful tree, was a part of the Amoeba, our ever-changing community of friends. Before long the pain and anguish that both Jon and I felt about that afternoon was absorbed by the Amoeba and transformed into laughter and forgiveness.

The word *community* comes from *communis*, the Old French and Latin word for sharing something—as in say, a common good. Whether based on a philosophical premise, like the community at a Zen monastery, or based on an experiment in living, like the Cornucopia commune or Walden, some communities share a way of thinking. People working on a PTA bottle drive or those involved in a business venture are temporary communities, formed simply to accomplish some task. Other communities are formed through cultural bonds. These can be very temporary, like the community of office mates singing Christmas carols, or deep-rooted, like the ties that bind people through common heritage. Still other communities are simply formed as a result of circumstances, the consequence of time and place. Of course, all these communities often overlap or change from one to another.

St. Johnsbury, where we raised our two sons, is a village of six thousand people who live along the banks of three small rivers in the northeastern corner of Vermont. Many of the people have lived there all their lives. Others are more recent arrivals. They work as loggers, waitresses, professors, and teachers. They work in stores, in social services, and in one or two of the small manufacturing companies nearby. Most of them worry about whether there is enough money, or how well their kids are doing in school, or if that big buck they saw last spring will still be around come hunting season. A small police force tries its best to keep up with domestic assaults, drug deals, and murder—crimes that are just as common here as in Anyplace, USA.

Our collars are white and blue and sometimes still tie-dyed in bright rainbow colors.

Because of its remoteness and the fact that it still has that white church steeple—Christmas card—Vermont look, the place has also attracted a high number of creative people. Writers and musicians, movie stars and filmmakers, artists and poets are also a part of the landscape. Like the rest of Vermont, the population is aging. Young adults, their eyes on something shinier than the dullness they see here, continue to flee the area, while retired refugees from the East Coast Megalopolis move in to take their place.

We moved to the town from the West before either of our children had started school. Soon after we arrived, we learned of a babysitting co-op. A group of twenty or so couples shared babysitting. The way it worked was you would earn points when you babysat for another member's kids. You could then spend those points by getting someone to watch your kids so that you and your spouse could have a nice evening out without having the expense of a babysitter. We were all of a certain age, with certain-aged children, and we all wanted to avoid paying for babysitters in order to save money. The co-op itself didn't work out well since some members were forever in debt—they always dodged having to babysit—while others horded their points and seldom went out even for a single evening. But the co-op did sow the seeds for a community of friends who, nearly thirty years later, still remain close. That group of couples (now supplemented by single men and women) still share much together. Sometimes as many as twenty or thirty of us will gather for dinner or a party; at other times, various smaller combinations will go on a hike or to a movie or will gather for an evening of games during the dark, dark winter nights. Some people have either moved away or simply drifted from the group, while newer friends have come along. Because of the shifting, imprecise shape of this loose gathering of locals, one friend has dubbed it the Amoeba.

While the Amoeba functions largely as a social gathering, it is also true we still act a little bit like the babysitting co-op. When someone needs help moving from one house to another, the Amoeba descends to lend their hands. That family in turn will join in when another member falls ill and needs help around the house. We bring in one another's firewood or show up when a house needs to be painted. We also know a great deal about one another's life history; we have met each other's in-laws and family, have attended the weddings of children, and often celebrate holidays together.

Unlike the commune movement of the 1960s, these friends don't share the same living space or constantly meet to discuss common issues. Still, decisions are frequently made in a collective manner. Everything, from the suggestion for a camping trip to the best way to help someone in trouble, is resolved by some nearly magical series of conversations, personalities, and shared resolve.

When we decided to build our house, Linda and I knew we wouldn't be able to do so without lots of help. My skills with a hammer (to say nothing about my skills with a chain saw) are limited. Books on building straw bale houses devote chapters to how much of the work can be done by friends. Well, only if your friends are talented, hardworking, and devoted.

Building a house was the most stressful thing I have ever done. Not good old-fashioned temporary stress but stress that stretched out over months and months, occupying every single waking moment. There was no leisure time that year. Because of the short building season, I was shackled to a very strict time schedule.

The most important event on that schedule was fast approaching. I had to have the post-and-beam framing in place by mid-July in order to be ready for the biggest and most complicated job of the entire construction project—the installation of the roof trusses.

The most critical factor—nay, my bene*factor*—in that undertaking was my friend Rick Stodola.

Rick works as an accountant, but he also has a reputation as a skilled carpenter. Modest and always able to create compromise and agreement, Rick is handier with a complicated building project than most people are with a keyboard. He had built everything from finely crafted furnishings to Habitat for Humanity houses.

Early on and for the length of the project, I sought Rick's advice. I based my plans, designed my schedule, and formed my budget around what he knew. I asked him every dumbbell question an English professor—turned—construction contractor might ask.

Rick explained that the roof trusses would be the single most labor-intensive part of the construction.

Trusses are large triangle-shaped structures that support the roof of a house. Take a cardboard box and imagine it as the frame for a house. Now take a bunch of Popsicle sticks and glue them into big triangles. Make twenty-six of them. Set one triangle after another across the narrow opening of the box and then secure them so that they stand upright, and you now have an idea of how trusses work. The difference, of course, was that my trusses were made out of milled lumber, and each weighed over one hundred pounds. Each one had to be placed perfectly upright ten feet in the air and then secured in just the right places, or else the finished roof might one day simply collapse.

It would be a monumental undertaking. I would need scissor lifts, ladders, and at least a dozen workers to help place, align, and secure each truss. Even if we were lucky and nothing went wrong, it would still take us eight to ten hours; and we had to be lucky, because there was only a single day, July 19, where everyone and everything would be available.

Oh yeah, I would also need a large crane to lift the trusses onto the roof.

As the Day of the Trusses approached, I withdrew into an extreme version of Automated Man. I became a man who saw to nothing but the complex arrangements and miniscule details of the task before me.

Luckily, there was the Amoeba. Rick and Jon weren't the only talented men in the nebulous group who had more skills and talent than I. At critical moments during the construction, these men always converged to help me. Many times, I would simply stand back in amazement at how four or five men, each a skilled craftsperson, could discuss, argue, and then agree on the proper way to accomplish a task.

The trusses, however, required more than just the talent and help of my friends; there was the matter of the crane. I knew it was going to cost a lot of money to rent one of the large machines. Also, I was having trouble finding any local contractors who were available that day. Then the Amoeba magic happened. One evening at our Victorian house there was a knock on the door. It was one of our neighbors who worked for a local excavator company.

"I hear you need a crane down at your new house," he said.

News of our project had spread through town. All sorts of friends and neighbors were interested in our work and often came to the site for a visit. I told him I sure did, and I explained that the deadline date was fast approaching.

"I've got nothing that Saturday; I'll bring the crane down there and help you out."

"You will?" I stammered. "That would be great!"

He turned to go. "What do you figure? About 6:00 a.m.?" he said over his shoulder.

"I've asked everyone to try to be ready by 7:30," I said. "Send me the bill; that way, I can get the bank to pay you quickly."

He waved a hand in the air. "You aren't going to pay me anything," he said. "No arguments."

There was no sustainable compromise when it came to the trusses. There was only one place that made them within five hundred miles. A manufacturer in Quebec, just north of the Vermont border, pretty much had the monopoly on building wooden trusses for every construction project around. The trusses arrived the day before we were to raise them. The driver who brought them to the site spoke only French, but I could tell he was in a horrible mood. It was raining miserably, and he barely acknowledged me, chain-smoking in the cold damp gray. He scrambled onto the hoist at the back of his big semi and dumped my trusses near the house site so rapidly that I thought I heard one crack. Sure enough, hours after he was safely back in Canada, I discovered that two of them had broken. I spent the darkening hours before T-Day hobbling two-by-four patches onto the broken trusses, alone in the pouring rain and crying.

I slept that night at the house site, where I awoke before first light and watched the dawn come brilliantly into a cool and crystal clear sky.

Just after sunrise my neighbor arrived with his crane on a flatbed truck. He parked and unloaded the big machine. Its tanklike treads clanked down the drive until it stopped at the pile of trusses. Then the others arrived: men and women and tools and ladders. One of my grown sons, who was visiting, arrived with two of his friends, a man and a woman who had moved to New Hampshire some years earlier and who had come back just to help us. My men friends came with their compressors and nail guns and know-how. Two or three of them were the conductors who figured out exactly who and why and when and what needed to happen. Over and over again, they explained to everyone just where to be and what to do.

In the preindustrialized countryside of Henry David Thoreau's time, neighbors commonly helped one another to accomplish such difficult tasks. Back then people routinely helped one another to plow, for example; and later in the season, they shared the work of reaping. They came together for larger projects or for heavy or tedious jobs such as raising a roof or husking corn. In these old-fashioned bees, people combined work and pleasure and created an intricate web of interdependence. But soon newfangled machines came along and required fewer people to operate them. Farmers could now do much of the work by themselves. At the same time, railroads and other improvements in transportation did away with the need to grow staples locally and further diminished cooperation

Fig. 5. The day of the roof trusses

Fig. 6. Parts of the Amoeba, July 4, 2007

and contact between neighbors. Gone was the work-together and play-together cohesiveness of community. That change in our cultural history was unfortunate, for such knowledge could help humanity in these coming difficult times. But the day of the trusses was nothing short of an old-style roof raising bee, courtesy of the Amoeba.

We started slowly. Someone attached the first truss to the crane with ropes and then signaled the driver. He lifted the huge triangle slowly into the air. Others supported it and guided it into place. Others were on ladders, ready to nail the truss into brackets that would attach it to the house frame. Still others were high above in the basket of a scissor lift, ready to plumb and secure the truss upright.

Even though it was a difficult and complex procedure, we soon fell into a pattern, each step being repeated in just the same sequence, until we all began to move like a single organism. Once in a while something halted us—moving ladders, fixing a not-quite-level truss, eating lunch. The work was difficult. People squeezed into tiny spaces or climbed with monkey-like courage high above on the bare skeleton of the roof. High in the air, suspended in awkward positions, they used circular saws or hammers, levels and nail guns. There were no hard hats.

Just before sunset we raised and secured the final truss. Soon after, most people went home. We loaded the crane back onto the truck and said inadequate thanks to our friends. A few stayed awhile longer, and we drank cold beer in the soft light of a summer dusk. We walked back and forth admiring our work, discussing the intricacies of an engineered design that could span a thirty-five-foot opening and yet hold an entire roof upright.

It was the Amoeba at its best.

Well, maybe second best. Our community of friends was most useful when the floor turned yellow.

A week after we installed the trusses and after some friends and I had finished putting on the metal roof, the house looked a lot like a pavilion one might see at picnic grounds: a roof supported by posts, covering a slab of concrete set in a green woods. That is when Harold, our concrete man, came back to color the slab floor.

We had decided not to cover the floor with carpets or wood so that the concrete could absorb more heat on sunny winter days. Concrete can be etched or cut, colored or acid stained so that it looks like tile or stone. We had decided to stain it to an earthy dark-brown color.

Harold had never used acid stain before, but he had attended workshops and talked often with another man who had done the process before.

He arrived to stain the floor, on a hot and humid morning. Linda was there, already nervous. We assured her that it was a straight-forward procedure and that there was nothing to worry about.

Harold filled a sprayer with a dark thick liquid the color of blood. He started in a corner of the slab, slowly spraying the acid in large swirling circles. After a few moments, he stopped and we all stared.

"It looks awful," Linda said.

Harold and I were speechless. The spray had turned the gray concrete into a sickly swirl of red-and-orange puke; at the edges of those splotches was yellow crud the color of mustard, French's yellow mustard.

"I'm sure it is going to be fine," Harold said. "We're doing everything right."

We?

"Don't worry," I stammered. "It'll look different after it sets a bit."

Harold fiddled awhile with the sprayer, adjusting the nozzle and pumping more air into it, before he began again. This time he worked for a long while without stopping. When he did stop, it was only to refill the sprayer with more stain.

"We shouldn't have done this," Linda said. "We should have used some other kind of floor."

I stormed away without responding. Half of me wanted to tell her to relax—this was just one more in a series of ongoing problems that building a house presented, and it would all work out fine. The other half of me was wracked by yet another sudden realization that I had made a monumental mistake, not just with the floor, but with the entire idea of building such an unusual house.

As soon as Harold finished, he packed up his gear and headed toward his truck. Linda was at his side, peppering him with a thousand questions. Why did it look so awful? What could be done? Could he call his friend and ask? What was going to happen next?

Harold hadn't seemed nervous before, but I could tell that Linda was getting to him. "I'm sure it will be fine," he said. "I'll come out tomorrow for a second coat."

"Do you think it will look better once it sets overnight?"

Harold leaned toward her and spoke as softly as he could. "Don't worry," he said again. "We are doing everything right." Then he climbed into his rig and was gone.

Linda didn't even look at me but simply stared at the floor and cried.

The day got worse. A realtor finally showed our Victorian house to someone that afternoon, but the people—flatlanders moving up from Massachusetts—didn't like the neighborhood. Adding to the horrible day was the fact that our dog was sick and dying; I had a flat tire on my truck; and it started to rain.

We went to bed that night without saying a word, each of us in a cloud of darkness.

In the morning, I had to deal with the flat tire and an emergency run to the vet, so Linda arrived at the land before I did. When I arrived, I knew instantly that things were bad. Linda and Harold were standing near the slab. Linda was speaking rapidly, leaning toward him and crying. Harold was nodding his head, opening his arms in a gesture of surrender.

I jumped out of the truck.

"What are we going to do about it? We can't leave it like this!" Her voice had the rare, strained quality of what she herself would call a major meltdown. She turned to look at me, but I was staring at the slab.

The floor of the entire house was now yellow—a sickly, yellow-matter-custard-dripping-from-a-dead-dog's-eye yellow.

While Harold continued to mumble how it would somehow work out, I moved quickly into that familiar, protective, nonemotional state, trying to ignore any attachment to the consequences of a permanently bright-yellow floor.

Linda, however, went from tears to anger to despair and finally to a woeful, wordless abandonment. "I have to leave," she sobbed, and got into her car.

"Honey," I said.

She jammed the car in reverse and raised her hand in the air. "I don't want to talk about it. I just want to leave."

She drove up the drive, and her car banged over a low spot before it disappeared in a cloud of dust.

I turned to Harold.

"It has to be some kind of by-product of the stain interacting with the concrete," he said.

"Can you call your friend who has done this before?"

"He's gone on a vacation. I won't be able to reach him for two weeks."

"Okay," I said.

"But I know we've done everything right . . ."

Harold was there to apply a second coat of stain. While he sprayed, I worked on framing the windows. Just before he finished, Linda returned, but she wasn't alone.

You guessed it: the Amoeba to the rescue.

Out of the car poured Linda and three of her women friends. They barely spoke to us but went immediately to inspect the slab. The women stood in a tight cluster of concern and words and, once or twice, short, soft laughter.

Harold quickly loaded his truck and left. I busied myself with the window frame.

In a little while the women came to where I was working. They spoke softly as if outside a hospital room where someone was gravely ill. They did not indicate me in this crisis, but somehow I felt indicated all the same. Finally one of them spoke to me directly.

"How's the rest of the work coming?" she said.

The women convinced Linda to take the rest of the day off. They drove away, headed for the beach at our local lake to bask in the sun, to swim, and to talk of husbands. When they returned a few hours later, I could tell that Linda was a bit better. She even smiled a small, pathetic, sad smile when I tried to joke that all we needed was to paint the house ketchup red to match the mustard-yellow floor.

During the next two, very tense days, the women of the Amoeba were everywhere in Linda's life. They showed up at the house site and talked about how carpets or throw rugs could help mask the disastrous floor. They took her to the movies. They invited her to dinner. They let her yell at them or call late at night in tears and rage; and with gentle hands, they caught their friend in the depth of her despair and set her back down again whole.

11

- - - - - - - -

The Straw That Broke The

When Harold showed up a couple of days later, he got down on his knees and spit on the concrete. He took out a rag and began to rub at the banana-yellow floor. He spit again. More rubbing.

He stood up.

"It's coming off," he said.

He was right: the yellow seemed to be a kind of powdery coating on the concrete, and underneath it was the earthy-brown color we had hoped to have.

"I'm on my way to another job site," he said. "You might try washing the floor to see how much more you can get off. That might put Linda at ease. I'll send out a crew with a power washer first thing tomorrow morning. It's going to be fine."

And it was fine. Although dubious, Linda spent that day with mops and water. Then the men came and, with high-pressured water, washed off the last of the yellow, exposing the beautifully marbled floor.

Linda, to say the least, was temporarily relieved.

Me, I didn't even have enough time to breathe a sigh of relief before I got a call from the farmer.

Ten months earlier I had called a dozen area farmers, trying to locate someone who could provide the straw bales. Armed with a list of questions, I quizzed each one about whether they had sold straw for house construction before (several had); what kind of string they tied the bales with (some materials are stronger than others for construction purposes); how they harvested their straw (if it was with a rotary blade, there might be more damage to the straw); how dense and how heavy the bales were; and, importantly, if they could store the bales until I needed them.

I chose an organic farmer whose farm was less than forty miles away. That would cut down on the cost of transporting the bales, and I liked that the straw would never have been exposed to pesticides and other chemicals.

The word *straw* dates back at least a thousand years to Old English. The word was used then, as now, to denote the stalk of cereal crops. But straw also used to mean, "to scatter something loosely about." Hence it was proper English to say that you *strawed* the baby powder or that the table had been *strawn* with cracker crumbs. Centuries later, when straw hats came into style, people often referred to them as your "straw."

Even in the old days the singular—one stalk—was called a straw. At some point early on, someone discovered you could use a straw to sip a drink. The "drinking straw" has been around for at least seven thousand years; but in the middle of the nineteenth century, it became fashionable for men to drink their rye whiskey using— you guessed it—a single straw of rye. Apparently, using the natural tube gave the whiskey a hint of the fresh flavor of the plant.

The problem with using a natural straw, however, is that before very long the thing begins to wilt and shred. In the 1880s, to combat this problem, a man invented a machine that wound paper into a tube. The paper straw was then coated with wax to make it last longer in a drink.

The stem of a stalk of straw is remarkably strong. Pay attention to the next patch of dry weeds you see. Those dead stalks are still standing because of their strength. Cellulose, a sturdy chemical molecule, forms the walls of the plant's cells. When packed into bales, the tough straw forms an incredibly durable and strong material. A bale of straw weighs around forty-five pounds if dry, closer to seventy if it isn't.

Straw is different from hay. Straw consists of the stalks that remain after grain has been harvested. Hay includes both the stalks and the seeds. You don't want to build a hay house, for the seeds might attract rodents and other pests.

Although the most common types of straw for building a house are wheat, oats, barley, and rye, many other kinds can be used. My organic farmer grew winter rye (*Secale cereale*), and that suited me fine. I also chose him over other local farmers because he had told me he'd store my bales until I needed them.

Or so I thought. Instead, a few days after the floor fiasco abated, he called, asking *where I wanted the bales delivered*. We had agreed that he would store the bales until I was ready for them, but the house wasn't ready yet. He denied that he had promised to store them. I told him that he had broken our agreement, but my anger was met only with a moment of silence from the other end of the line. "I have the bales," he said. "If you don't want them, let me know."

I had no options. It was too late to find another farmer. Not only did I suddenly have to find a place large enough to store the bales, but it also had to be dry and close to the house site. I had to set aside everything else in order to deal with this new problem.

The situation also meant I would have to move the bales not once but twice. I had calculated I would need around 275 bales for the house. That figures out to 12,375 pounds, or roughly six tons. I would need over 1,500 cubic feet of storage area that could hold such a weight and was also dry and cool; and I would need nearly a full day and a crew of three able-bodied people each time I moved them.

I took another deep breath, ignored the voices in my head that screamed how insane this entire thing was, and began.

I asked a colleague of mine who owned a barn five miles from our house site if he could store the bales. He said the barn had a lot of old stuff in it; but if I would help him clean it out, he'd rent it to me for $100. I spent a day cleaning out old lumber, horse harnesses, tractor parts, ancient kids' toys, Model A crank starters, a 1930s-era picnic table, buggy wheels, tractor wheels, other indeterminable wheels and cranks, coal and grease buckets, and more. We swept out years of dirty, dusty straw and debris, fixed a door hinge that had fallen off, and secured the ramp well enough to support new traffic. I found a couple of teenaged boys who agreed to load the bales, possibly because their mother convinced them that their summer wasn't going to be spent sitting in front of a screen all day long and that they were going to do some actual work for some actual pay. I called the farmer; and a few days later, the boys and I and a worker from the man's farm off-loaded the bales from the farmer's trailer and into the barn.

Now behind schedule even more, I rushed to complete everything that needed to be in place before the crew I had hired to build the straw part of the house arrived. As per their instructions, I ordered sand and lime and rented a huge generator and water hoses. I covered the new and now beautiful floor with paper to protect it, insulated the beam, and tried to finish all the things that absolutely had to be finished before the builders came. Amid this week or two of chaotic eighteen-hour days, the old and loveable family dog was getting worse, screaming (there is no other word) in pain in the middle of the night and collapsing onto the floor; we endured a hot, thunderous evening of tornado warnings and hail; and we watched a small handful of potential buyers visit our old house and then ask our realtor what else she might have to show them.

One day at dawn, I picked up the two teenaged helpers I had hired. We drove to the barn in the early morning light, while I unsuccessfully tried to make small talk with these two adolescent boys who had been awakened in the wee hours on a summer vacation day to once again endure hard labor for some gray-bearded loon.

The owner of the barn had loaned me his dump truck and a large trailer, and they were parked near the barn, waiting for us. One teen climbed into the barn and up to the top of the huge stack of bales and tossed or handed or rolled bale after bale to us. The other boy and I stood below, hefting each bale and walking it out to the rigs. I had to supervise loading the wagon as well, explaining to the teens how to stack the bales so that they would not fall off. The sun cracked the sky with early heat. There was no dew on the grass, and already sweat soaked our T-shirts. We worked through the morning, as I watched the mammoth pile of bales in the barn barely diminishing. The woman who rented the farmhouse came out with her four children to watch us as we moved, ant-like from straw to truck to barn to straw to truck, stopping briefly for a break of water and apples and then back to loading the straw.

By noon the temperature had climbed nearly to ninety; by two, when we finally drove the rigs down to the house site, it was ninety-five.

If the boys were exhausted—and the slumped shoulders, downcast heads, and eagerness to pause in their work seemed to indicate that they most certainly were—then this man, who was forty years their senior, must have been near death. The sun was directly over our heads. In slow motion, we grabbed bale after bale from the truck and trailer and lugged them under the shelter of the pavilion-like structure that was to become our home. We did not speak, only uttering an occasional grunt when meeting with an unruly or particularly heavy bale. On and on into the blistering afternoon we labored, moving increasingly slower as the heat and the exhaustion beat us down.

Finally, it was done. I returned the dump truck and trailer and took the boys home just as the sun finally began to cool in the early evening. Some zombie form of myself got me back to the house site and then sat motionless on the concrete floor. The stack of bales nearly filled the interior. I stared blankly at them. Nothing registered anymore, not the straw, not the heat, not the progress I had made building the house, and most of all not my aching, exhausted body and automated heart.

12

- - - - - - - - - -

Finances

Then there came the Great Recession of 2007. On July 19, the day our trusses arrived from Canada, the Dow closed at over fourteen thousand for the first time in history. By early August, about the time I was loading and reloading the straw with the boys, the worldwide credit crunch began. Lenders all over the globe stopped offering home equity loans. The construction of our new house was reaching its peak, and we weren't getting any nibbles on our old house. On August 6, the day the workers arrived to start building the straw walls, American Home Mortgage Company became the first of many such organizations to file for bankruptcy. Within months, the Dow would tumble to half its size.

Then the real estate bubble popped so loudly you could hear it from our Vermont hills all the way to the banks of Iceland.

In March, when we first listed it with a realtor, our Victorian house was one of only eleven residential properties for sale in town. By October, when we took it off the market, there were seventy-eight houses for sale; and nothing, nothing, nothing was selling.

Getting a construction loan for our house hadn't been simple. Although straw bale houses have been financed using the federal Fannie Mae guidelines, obtaining a construction loan for our house involved a lot of work and luck. Even in the heady times just before the bubble burst, bankers were conservative in their loans. Since a house won't have any resale value until it is completed, a bank's money is at a very high risk when it is tied up in the construction loan. Any construction project was a risk; and because ours was out of the ordinary, not many banks were willing to take us on.

We soon learned not to begin by telling a bank's loan officer that we intended to build a straw bale house. When we did, she or he immediately asked us if we knew about the three little pigs. We would have to smile and act as if we hadn't already heard that joke hundreds of times already. We learned instead to tell them that we planned on using alternative building materials for part of our house. When the subject of straw finally came up, we were well armed with materials. I had documents from the U.S. Department of Energy and other governmental agencies that spoke positively about straw bale construction. I had data on the increasing number of such homes. I explained that several states had building codes just for straw bale houses and that although Vermont was not one of them, we were going to build our house to the standards of those codes. I developed a thorough and detailed budget for our house. I had gotten bids on everything from the foundation to the roof. I had statistics on resale values and straw bale house longevity. And I learned to laugh loudly when the story of the first little pig was told.

We received a construction loan, but payments on it were steep. The idea is to build the house as quickly as possible and then turn the construction loan into a mortgage at a much lower rate. Our plan was to sell our old house, use that money to pay down the new straw bale house mortgage, and *presto*, achieve financial stability in a sustainable, energy-efficient home. Then everyone everywhere stopped buying houses, and we were stuck with both: one fine old Victorian house and one half-finished house of straw.

We will now discuss how house construction and its attendant finances place considerable strain on a marriage.

Fig. 7. The author at work

The tension manifested itself in many ways. I'd grow angry at Linda's insistence on knowing every little detail of what had to be done and why. She'd grow frustrated with my silence and lack of communication. I'd go nearly crazy at how she would take it on herself to do what I saw as some little, needless chore while so much else needed doing. She had never seen me so bossy or aloof in our thirty years together.

One night during the floor fiasco, we were driving back to the old house, when we snapped. We had been talking about some frustration from the day, when I tossed a small Molotov cocktail.

"I ask you to do one thing, and you want to do another," I said.

Linda's voice got that slow and terse tone that meant she was very angry and upset. "I can't understand why you just won't let me work at things my way . . ." she said.

"It's not efficient," I said.

". . . and you don't share things with me," she continued, her voice rising. "I don't know what is going on."

"The more I share with you, the more you worry. And the more you worry, the harder it is for me to do things. Then I have to have conversations like this."

"'Like this'?" She burst into tears. "How else am I supposed to know about things? It makes me feel worthless and not a part of decisions."

Then, out of nowhere, I lobbed the first thermonuclear device. "You didn't have to make such a big deal about the floor," I hissed. "Now the entire town is talking about it."

There ensued such tears and rage and anger and finally as cold and black a silence as few have ever seen. What Linda had to deal with, of course, was a manic, soulless man. Deep at the center of it all were my own weaknesses and fear. I walked a razor's edge between the black resignation of absolute doubt and the equally dark pit of blind overconfidence. Even if I had not already turned myself into an emotionless automated machine, my curt, rude treatment of her was despicable.

Such tensions between us found only small avenues of release, each of us finding solace in the intimacy of a close friend or in solitude or in silent anger. Once in a while we would stop at the end of a day and praise each other for what we had accomplished, or we would stand a long while, embracing in silence. I'd get weepy and apologize for being so incompetent, worried that I was in way over my head. She'd try to buoy me up and act as if it was all one big adventure.

I suppose we were seeking what had always saved the love and friendship that has been our marriage: a sustainable compromise. She tried to forgive me my bad behavior, and I tried to not care about hers.

As far as I can determine, the year I spent at the yurt, I lived on a measly $1,200. Most of that, $79 a month, went to land payments. The cost of food made up the rest. I had no health insurance, no rent, no utility bills, and no car. On the rare occasions I needed a phone, I hiked out to the highway and hitched a ride ten miles to use the pay phone in the small village of Cerrillos. Every few weeks, my friend Brenda would appear and take me into Santa Fe for a night out. A common treat was to eat at Furr's Cafeteria, a buffet-style restaurant that had every home-style food a man could want, from meat loaf to pumpkin pie.

If it hadn't been for those rare car trips to town, I would not have known about the economic crisis that was then sweeping the world. It was the start of the world's oil crisis. In a four-month period, beginning the summer I built the yurt, oil prices *quadrupled*, forever ending the luxury of cheap energy.

According to a report from the Shorenstein Program in Politics, Policy, and Values at UC Berkeley, in October 1973 Arab members of OPEC raised the price of crude oil by 70 percent and placed an embargo on exports to the United States and other nations allied with Israel. "Although the fighting ended in late October, OPEC continued to use the 'oil weapon' over the coming months," the

report states. "In November oil exporters cut production 25% below September levels, and the following month they doubled the
price of crude. By January 1974 world oil prices were four times
higher than they had been at the start of the crisis."

The oil crisis had a profound impact on the international system. The crisis worsened the economic difficulties that were then
facing the industrialized nations of the West. The increased energy prices slowed economic growth and caused inflation—a combination that came to be known as "stagflation." And the UC Berkeley report argues that "by putting an end to decades of cheap oil,
the crisis forced industrialized nations to seek ways to curb their
energy use. In the U.S. this led to such measures as gas rationing
and the adoption of a national 55 mile per hour speed limit." Just
being able to pay for getting to and from work suddenly became
a reason why people had to work even more.

None of this mattered a whit to me. "Lo!" Thoreau wrote, "Men
have become the tools of their tools." Not I, whose simple life and
volunteer poverty freed me from being affected by the events
of the world. Naïve, yes; selfish, perhaps; but that simplicity and
the closeness of the natural world allowed me to contemplate my
journey itself and not to spend my days laboring for money, with
distant and dim hopes for the freedom to one day live such a life.

13

- - - - - - - - - -

Collaboration

It's not like I had a lot of money in those days anyway. When I was hired to teach at the Tesuque school, the September before I built the yurt, the community told us—even at only $5 a day—it might be a month before we got our first pay. It didn't matter. None of the teachers were there for the money. Some, like a former Peace Corp volunteer, were there out of a dedication to helping the poor, voiceless ones in society; other teachers, like the married couple who were hired, had kids in the school; others, like me, had the idealistic goal of being able to educate young people for the betterment of society; and some teachers were motivated by a reaction to the corrupt political system that caused the creation of the school in the first place.

The previous spring, the superintendent of the Santa Fe School District had pushed a bond vote on the town. He said the bond money would be used to build a new north-side elementary school outside the city limits. In private he told the leaders of Tesuque and two smaller neighboring villages that their old school would be torn down and that the money would be used to build the new school *at the same location in Tesuque*. The bond issue passed, but almost immediately the idea of a new school took a backseat to other budgetary concerns. Rumors had it that the superintendent had all along planned on building the new school *in Santa Fe*, in a new, high-end housing development. Shortly thereafter, in what would eventually be determined to have been an illegal vote, the Santa Fe School Board closed the Tesuque school. The only dissenting board member, a dentist, feebly objected, since the numbers didn't indicate that the school needed to be closed. By four to one, the board voted to close the last rural school in Santa Fe County—a county larger than the state of Rhode Island.

"We don't have anything against busing the students," a vocal Tesuque community member said. "It isn't a long ride to town. We just believe that our children belong here, in our village. We want them here so that we can see after their education. If they go to Santa Fe, they will be put into classrooms that are already overcrowded. Here, they are still our children."

The unity in the community was astounding. Nearly every family with children in the elementary school defied the school board's actions. The few that didn't—one woman who worked in the school system and another family that currently held the school system's busing contract—were understandable exceptions.

Shortly after the villages announced that they intended to start their own school, I hitched a ride out to Tesuque in order to apply there to teach.

Cars were parked in front of the school building when I arrived on a midafternoon in late August. The front door of the building was open. I walked in. A couple of kids raced past me through the doors. Others were sitting quietly in the hallway, talking and playing.

Inside a room, a handful of women sat at a table. Some were typing; two others were on phones. No one noticed my entrance.

A slender woman hung up the phone. She walked over to me. "Can I help you?" she said, not impolitely. The room grew silent. The others had finally noticed me and had stopped working.

"I came to apply for a teaching job," I said.

The work resumed on the table.

"Oh good," the slender woman said. Her hair was pulled back thinly against her head and tied in the back with a rubber band. "My name is Mollie Freeman," she said, extending her hand. "I am, well, I guess I am the principal of the new school."

She explained the situation to me. The parents of Tesuque and two neighboring villages decided that their children would not be getting on the school buses when school started the following week. Instead, somehow, somewhere, they would have their own school. The parents were united in their resolve, no matter what happened. The Santa Fe school system was going to lose out on a lot of federal and state money without those students, and they would not be happy.

A phone rang. "Mollie," someone said.

She took a sheet of paper off the table and handed it to me. "I'm sorry, but things are a bit chaotic right now. Here, we've been using this as an application." She turned back toward the table.

"Ah, this is a blank sheet of paper," I said.

She waved her hand in the air, reaching for the phone. "Just write all the information you think we need to know about you," she said.

I walked out of the room and went into one of the classrooms. I found a pencil and looked at the blank sheet of paper. That totally blank sheet was, and still remains, the oddest job application form I have ever filled out. I wrote my name. My address. I wrote down my college education and listed my very limited previous teaching experience. Four lines. Maybe I could write really big and fill the page. I began to explain how I felt about education, about the way teaching and learning had to be cooperative, something that happened not only between student and teacher but between the teachers and the parents and between the students as well.

I was almost finished, when there was a roar of activity outside the room. Mollie sped past the door, did a double take as if remembering me, and then stuck her head in the room.

"Don't rush," she said, "but when you are finished, just put your application on the table in the other room." She looked out the windows nervously. "I'm sorry to be so distracted, but we just got a call. The trucks are coming to clean out the building. The school district is going to take everything: the desks, the books, everything." She turned toward the door and then looked at me. "But we aren't going to let them." And then, as an afterthought, she said, "You might not want to be here when they arrive—it could be ugly."

Choice time.

I hesitated only a second. "Do you want some help?" I asked, and followed her into the hall.

The halls were a whirl of women and children. People were scattering out over the entire building. Some positioned themselves in front of bookcases; others sat on teacher's desks.

"The piano!" Mollie shouted. "That piano was donated to the school by Mary Ann. We can't let them get the piano!" She turned to me. "Oh, we don't have enough people to hold onto everything."

"Why don't I just stand in front of the main doors?" I said.

Mollie looked at me for only a moment. "That is very nice," she said, "but you don't have to get involved. We are going to keep our school. Everyone who is staying here is a part of our community. You could get in big trouble."

I shrugged. "Go protect that piano," I said. "I'll be outside."

I went outside and closed the big double doors of the schoolhouse behind me. The warm, dry late-summer sun felt good. Through the trees, I could see a few huddled adobe houses on a hill. I could hear the sound of a small river. Beyond the houses, the Sangre de Cristo Mountains rose gently toward the blue. I could hear birds.

Two white moving vans slowed down and then turned into the drive. They pulled straight up to the door and then stopped. Men got out. They were big and strong and not friendly looking.

They came up to me. The largest one spoke. "Hello," he said.

"Howdy," I answered.

"We're from the school district," he said. "We came to clear out the school."

"I know," I said.

The men looked at one another. I stood with my hands behind me, clenching the door handles with my sweating fists.

They formed a small, tight circle around me. Another man spoke. "We have to get to work now," he said, but none of us moved.

Just then, a state patrol car pulled into the drive, followed by the county sheriff.

"Ah shit," someone said.

The cops walked up to us. They looked at the trucks, then at the men, and finally at me.

The state patrolman spoke to me. "Okay, what's going on here?"

"These guys are coming to clear out the building," I said.

"And you?"

"I'm blocking the door."

Two of the men laughed.

The cops hesitated for a moment. I could tell they were trying to decide what to do. It is always the *unplanned* moments of choice that determine our future. It is then that we most need sustainable compromises.

Someone pushed at the doors from the inside, trying to get out.

Mollie appeared behind me. "We are getting a court injunction to prevent the school district from touching anything."

The movers looked relieved.

"But you don't have it yet?" the sheriff spoke.

I pressed myself harder against the doors.

"We'll have it first thing in the morning," Mollie said.

"Listen honey," the sheriff said, "if there's no court injunction, then you are preventing these men from doing their jobs."

"Well, *honey*," Mollie said, "we will have one by 8:00 a.m. tomorrow." Before anyone could say a word, she added, "There's a fresh pot of coffee; anyone want some?" She shouted back into the school. "Henrietta, bring out some coffee and a bunch of cups."

A moment later a woman appeared with coffee and a huge plate of home-baked chocolate chip cookies. The men who had come to move the equipment out of the school turned and then sat on the steps. The story of the parents' defiance was well-known; and despite the fact they worked for the school system, it was clear the men were on the parents' side. We sat down beside them, while the two cops just watched. The conversation was polite at first; we all talked about the dry weather, the recent heat spell, and each other's plans for Fiesta weekend.

Then it got down to business. The men had a job to do. Their superiors knew they were sending them to do a thankless task, but their bosses were back in Santa Fe in their air conditioned offices. "We don't want to do this," the men said over and over, "but we have to. They might fire us if we don't bring stuff back."

"I have an idea," someone finally said. "Why don't you just take all the useless stuff—you know, the trash cans, maybe the mops and janitorial supplies, there's a broken table I noticed, and some extra playground equipment."

The men thought a moment and then grinned. "By the time we get back, it will be time to quit for the day."

"And by tomorrow we'll have the injunction," Mollie said.

Soon the state policeman left. The sheriff stayed only a little while longer, watching us load a large barrel of floor wax into one of the vans. When we had finish loading the trucks with useless things, there was another round of coffee before the men climbed in their rigs.

"Thank you," someone said to them.

"We are glad to help you people," the large man said from the cab of his truck. "Don't let them close your school. Stand up for what is yours." He started the truck. "*Vaya con Dios*," he said, and drove away.

Of the forty or so people who had applied to teach at the parents' school, I was among the seven who had been selected to be interviewed. I was told to be at the school at seven o'clock one evening. Someone would be there to take me to the interview.

A friend dropped me off at the abandoned building at a quarter till. I wore the only dress-up clothes I owned: a clean, good shirt and corduroy pants. I stood in the empty parking lot waiting. A little past seven a pickup truck swung into the lot. A thirty-something handsome Chicano was at the wheel. He stopped and rolled down the window. "Can I help you?" he asked.

"That's okay," I said, "I'm just waiting for a ride. I'm here about teaching."

The man grinned. "Jump in. I'm on my way to the meeting myself."

I climbed in. We shook hands. "I'm Juan Romero," he said. "I'm the president of the new school group." He reached below the seat and pulled out two cans of beers. He opened one and offered me the other.

I took it. Not bad, I thought. The president of the school group and I were sharing a beer. A beer? On the way to a job interview?

Ten minutes later we were bouncing up a dusty back road that led past a handful of small adobe houses. We pulled to a stop near one of the houses. Cars and trucks filled the yard.

Juan grabbed the remainder of the six-pack and jumped out. I followed him into the house.

"Juan," someone said, "it's good to see that the president could make it!"

Juan laughed and shook hands.

I quickly took a seat on the floor near the fireplace and waited. The small living room was packed with people. Most of them were Hispanic, although there were also a number of Anglos. I began to pick out the others who were here to be interviewed to teach.

Juan started the meeting by tapping a spoon against his beer can.

I watched that evening progress in silent amazement. There was neither agenda nor formality but rather some magical force by which everyone seemed to come together.

After a little while, Juan turned to a massively built man who had been standing silently in a corner.

"People," Juan said, "this is Father Ben. If you don't already know, Father Ben is our new priest at the church."

Father Ben stepped forward, a can of beer in one hand. "I am here to offer the church as a place for the village school," he said.

From there, the evening seemed more like one long conversation than like a meeting. Somebody would say something; then there would be a moment of silence before another person would speak. After a while people simply came to an agreement about what had to be done and whose responsibility it would be to make it happen. The room was fogged in with the smoke of cigarettes.

People offered what they could contribute or how they might help with things like tents for more classroom space, chemical toilets, books, school supplies, chalk, lunches for one hundred kids, and so on. It seemed as if a thousand decisions were being made that night, with fair debate and without rancor. Juan stood all night, summarizing each discussion; and then, almost as an intrusion, there would be a vote.

The teachers were saved for last. Finally, we each were asked to stand and say something about ourselves. One by one we spoke. Juan asked us all to step outside for a while. Ten minutes later we were called back inside. All seven of us had been hired.

In the coming months, I watched as the people of three small New Mexican villages set aside race and wealth, old grudges and newly minted offenses to create a vibrant, successful school out of absolutely nothing.

Collaboration, the ability to work together, was essential to the success of the school. Clearly the urgency of the decisions and of the work that had to be done contributed to their ability to collaborate. Surely everyone's strong commitment to keeping the school open helped as well. Still, there had to be something more going on in order for those widely divergent people to work together so harmoniously. In the months that followed, it became clear to me that these people had overcome the usual impediments to accomplishing a difficult task, over a long period of time. The school was incredibly successful, because every person set aside personal pride for community pride, selfishness for magnanimity, and, perhaps hardest of all, the need to always appear right.

How can we keep alive the desire and the dream that in our striving for an ideal community, we will transcend the overwhelming evidence of the baseness of human nature? "How to love," Dorothy Day wrote, "that is the question." Although the times are dark and the desert we pass through is bleak, hope should never be abandoned, she said, because in every person, there is something "which is of God." Just look to the poorest among us, she claimed; just look at the poorest and most destitute among us, and you will find transcendence in their desire to create communities of mutual help and protection. To meet the future requires an act of faith, and "faith, like love, is an act of the will, an act of preference."

The idea of working together for a common goal, even though the people involved might not ever otherwise form a community, makes a lot of sense. We often share the same goals as other people

Fig. 8. The straw house takes shape

but lack enough tools or talent or knowledge to accomplish them by ourselves. Today, the idea of collaboration is everywhere. Regional hospitals work together in order to share services and doctors; schoolteachers collaborate, leaning on one another's skills in order to better educate their students; and corporations, town governments, and many other organizations have jumped on the bandwagon. Possibly no other area has more companies touting themselves as collaborative than the alternative-construction industry. The company I hired to help build the straw bale part of my house, for example, was called GreenSpace Collaborative.

The crew from GreenSpace was due to arrive on a Monday in early August. Sure enough, just after dawn I heard the roar of a truck driving up the road. In a moment, an ancient International Harvester—a big, boxy pickup the size of a Hummer—bounced down the drive and pulled up to where I stood next to the house. The engine coughed once and then slowly died in a cloud of blue smoke that smelled of hamburgers.

Out jumped a medium-sized man about thirty-five. He had piercing, friendly eyes and an earnest, sincere smile. He introduced himself as Daniel.

After a little small talk, I couldn't help myself. I asked him about the strange smell. He opened the camper shell on the back of the truck. Inside was a large tank connected to pipes and strange mechanics. He had converted the old truck to run on vegetable oils, which he got for free from fast-food restaurants. Last winter, he told me, he had driven the truck all the way to the tip of Baja Mexico and back again on nothing but free fuel.

Twenty minutes later, Andy arrived.

Andy was the main owner of GreenSpace. The business had been launched in 1996 to integrate green site design and construction. Many of the company's projects were centered on straw bale construction in the Northeast. Andy had taken over the company two years earlier.

The idea behind the business was to produce economically and ecologically sound houses by using a team of workers from a variety of professions. To do this Andy gathered crews with different skills depending on the project. In addition to his construction crew, he contracted with professionals in the fields of energy-systems engineering, renewable energy, and building-science technology. Ideally, this type of collaboration also meant trying to work with similar and often competing construction companies. The concept means that if Company A needed a special piece of equipment, they would be able to borrow it from Company B, even though Company B was a direct competitor for other contracts. Company B, in turn, would feel fine about using the skills or equipment of Company A at a later date.

In theory this works fine and everyone benefits. The trouble comes, as it always seems to do, from competition. I had gotten bids from two other straw bale construction companies before I se-

Fig. 9. The interior of the house during the straw bales phase

lected Andy's. Now those companies were supposed to loan their expertise (and get less pay) or their equipment (putting it out of service for their own use) to help their direct competitor become more successful. It was a tenuous arrangement. In the end, Andy did not ask for help from these other companies.

Before the day was out, three other workers arrived. Two of them, a young man and woman, had just graduated from Hampshire College, which specialized in alternative education with an experimental curriculum. They were anxious to put into action their ideals of building a sustainable building. The third, also a young man, was the type of strong and capable worker you are very happy to have on a job. Their final worker, the one with the least talent or skill, was me.

For the next ten days, I worked alongside this crew, as we cut and shaped bales to build the walls of my house. Slowly, I got a picture of how collaboration, cooperation, and commitment could help sustain human life in the coming decades.

For one thing, these people made few compromises with their ideal of leaving a small carbon footprint. From Daniel's biodiesel truck to everyone's desire to camp on my land rather than waste resources by taking a motel room, they practiced what they preached. They showered with water from a solar-heated shower bag and ate meals prepared from veggies purchased at a local farmer's stand. Although I thought I was building with environmental awareness, these folks made me acutely aware of the compromises I had made.

But there is hope. Even for me. We can change.

Writer Diane Ackerman has researched the latest scientific evidence of how the human brain works. "The brain is constantly rewiring itself based on daily life," she writes. "In the end, what we pay most attention to defines us. How you choose to spend the irreplaceable hours of your life literally transforms you." If we spend the irreplaceable hours of our lives in competition, selfishness, and greed, well then we become selfish and greedy, and the world suffers.

Hope comes again within the practice of deep ecology—being aware of the implications of our own actions in *all* aspects of our life. If we spend our hours in cooperation, awareness, and collaboration, then we survive.

14

Artifacts

Years after I left New Mexico for good, I visited the site of the yurt on a summer vacation, from Vermont, with Linda and the boys. Naturally, I had to show my sons the place where the old man once lived a hermit's life.

It had been over twenty-five years since I built the yurt. The road from Santa Fe had changed, of course; now fancy haciendas (most of them, large wood-framed things, plastered and stained to approximate the look of a real adobe house) were scattered over the hillsides. Several miles before Madrid, dark low trees sheltered a house and a handful of buildings that could have been the site of the Cornucopia commune, but I couldn't remember the location for certain.

From there to Madrid the road was now littered with houses and dirt roads that disappeared over hills to more houses, all-terrain vehicle tracks, and mailboxes. Several little, boxy ranch-style homes were surrounded by ticky-tacky pole fences made to resemble the kind you might have found decades ago on a real ranch. Home after home, separated via some zoning foresight by an acre or two, appeared right up until we drove around the last curve to the town of Madrid.

Madrid. What had once been nothing but a handful of ramshackle buildings, nearly blown away by time, was now a living community.

Founded in 1869, Madrid started its first boom in the 1890s, when the world began to demand the coal buried beneath the town. The mine shaft went deeper and deeper, and the town's population grew to at least three thousand. By 1906 Madrid was a company town. The town and the seams of coal beneath it were all owned by the Albuquerque and Cerillos Coal Company. For the dangerous job of mining coal, the company provided a tiny house to each miner and a store where they could get supplies on credit. The men worked long hours in extremely hazardous conditions and "bought" their groceries with company "money." They often ended up owing all of each week's wages to the company. Those conditions improved under the leadership of a more civilized superintendent who took over in the 1920s. Oscar Huber paved the streets and sidewalks of the town, built a school for the children, and even added a small hospital. Electricity was free and created via the town's own generating station.

In 1936 Huber gained controlling interest in the town and mine, but Madrid's heyday had passed. When natural gas began to compete with coal in the early 1950s, people left the company and the company-owned houses, tavern, and store. The mining operation shut down. Soon the town was nothing but dusty, weed-choked streets and broken windows.

By the late 1960s the town was under the ownership of Huber's son. There was nothing left of Madrid but empty buildings and rows of small wooden houses slowly disappearing to time. Huber's son placed an ad in the *Wall Street Journal*, offering to sell the entire town—over one hundred houses, a dozen large buildings, and one large coal mine—for $250,000.

When I first saw Madrid in the early 1970s, there were rumors the Walt Disney Company was interested in buying it for a movie set, but the town did not sell. Finally the owner decided to sell or rent individual buildings. The advent of an alternative lifestyle—back to the land, beautiful-loser types like me—fit precisely with this man's desire to reap some benefit from his father's investment. A person could buy a house, albeit a derelict, isolated, ghost-town house, for $50. The second boom to hit Madrid happened just as I left the yurt.

Into the tiny clapboard and framed houses where the families of miners once tried to find happiness in a world full of toil and troubles, long-haired dreamers now moved. Although often destitute, they brought with them a hope against all evidence that they could make a better world. Instead of pickax and coal dust, these men and women labored with pottery wheel or water colors, with cantankerous ancient John Deere tractors or vw microbuses, with feeding the kids and trying to survive—in short, with the simple essentials of living.

Slowly the town came back to life. Today, Madrid touts its unique history. In addition to the Coal Mine Museum, the town brags about being a community of artisans. A casual look tells you that the place is unique. Houses made from old railroad boxcars, or stained glass embedded in an ancient wooden gate, or any one of a thousand other artifacts says something meaningful about the town. Before anyone had ever heard of recycling or sustainability, these people knew it is wiser and cheaper to reuse materials already close at hand. They had wisdom as old as the hills; for as anyone who has had to live on little money knows, you find a use for everything and you waste nothing.

We were just crossing the big arroyo south of Madrid when things finally began to feel familiar. "This is more what things looked like back then," I told the boys with a wave of my hand. On the hillside were rows of wooden shacks that had once served as the homes of the miners and their families. Most were not much larger than a single car garage, while others had been expanded with small additions and porches. Now many were clothed in pale-colored vinyl siding, while still others looked as if nothing

Fig. 10. The straw bale house under construction

had been done to them since the 1970s: brown wood siding the color of coffee, small windows, and a dull tin roof.

People in the building trade are well aware of the costs of wasted materials. Ideally, you try to build an entire house without having a scrap of unused material left over. When I designed and built the straw bale house, I tried to be very conscious of waste. For one thing, I tried to design my house using standard-sized materials. I could use standard-length studs for my interior walls, for example. That way, I never had to shorten a longer piece to a nonstandard length—hence no waste. Other products like Sheetrock and foam board come in standard sizes too, so I designed the size of things to fit them. While it's difficult to build a new home without waste, my sustainable compromise was to be continually aware of the problem and to constantly limit what I threw away.

Even though I carefully considered the problem, by the time we finished the straw bale house, we still had generated a fair bit of trash. What couldn't be recycled or reused, we either took to the dump or threw in one of the biodegradable waste piles we created not far from the house site. Most of the waste was wood scraps, piles of straw, and other materials; but in one pile, we put things that might last a little longer, like concrete. You end up wasting concrete on any big job because often leftover cement has to be dumped or else it can ruin the truck. There wasn't a great deal of concrete waste, but what there was now sits at the bottom of a slope not far from the house. On top of the concrete are the less green wastes I tossed away: boards with nails still in them, shreds of tar paper, a pair of ruined cotton work gloves, and entire wooden pallets. Blackberries and brambles have made my waste piles all but invisible, and slowly, but perceptibly, they are disappearing back into the earth.

We had the good fortune to live close to a store that sold a wide assortment of used and salvaged building materials. It was located in an old warehouse in a nearby town. Doors, windows, hinges, nails, electrical fixtures, fancy trim, and even the Greek style columns from an old church were all there to be had. I found a couple of perfectly fine cabinets for next to nothing, as well as the exterior trim for our windows. I also purchased several long slabs of marble for under $50. One piece now serves as the bar top for our kitchen island, and the other caps the half wall that defines a small hallway.

Our straw bale home is full of such relics.

When I needed something to use for door handles on our screen porch, I remembered having seen an old piece of farm equipment rusting away in the woods above the house.

One evening, I walked up there to see if I could reuse any of it. The dilapidated machine was sheltered by a couple of maples that grew out of the cellar hole of a long-ago abandoned building. It was a wooden wagon of some kind; but instead of a flat bed, it had a hopper with the rusted remnants of mechanical contraptions attached. I later learned the old machine was a McCormick Number Four Ensilage and Forage Blower. The device was made in 1956 and was one of the last farm implements ever built that could be either pulled by a tractor or hitched behind a team of horses.

Armed with a wrench, pliers, and a couple of beefy screwdrivers, I circled the old wreck like a butcher, looking for the best place to cut. Square and wagon-sized, it had chains and little metal buckets; and up near the remains of a wooden seat, a brake handle poised and ready to be used. As interesting as all these things were, I still hadn't found anything that I could use as door handles. I stopped to inspect an axle of some kind. At either end was a long metal tube with a grease cup on the top. Each metal cup was about the size and shape of a large shot glass and had a metal cap covering the top. You would screw off the cap and then fill the cup full of grease. Gravity then fed the grease down the tube to the axle. I stood and stared at them. *Yes!* The perfect door handles.

On the way back through the woods, I felt the tiniest cringe of pothunter guilt, as if I had ransacked some archeological treasure for my own gain; but I shook that off as I studied my plunder and saw how perfectly they would work.

As soon as I got back to the house site, I unscrewed the caps. I scraped out big globs of fifty-year-old grease, chocolaty dark in color and as thick as peanut butter. I poured some gasoline into a small bucket and used it to clean them. As I splish-splashed in the gasoline bath, delighted with my find and smugly patting myself on the back for being so green, I suddenly realized how I compounded things. How do I dispose of the dirty gasoline, the rags, and all that grease? Sure, it isn't but a quart of gas and no more grease than what might ooze off my truck in just a few months of sitting in the drive; but since my mind had been working on the ethics of my actions, it became a central question: how do I dispose of this dirty gasoline and this grease?

I put the grease and the rags in a bag that I would take to the town dump, and the gas I tossed into the trash wood pile on top of the discarded concrete, falsely assuring myself it would be the best thing I could do with it.

The incident caused me to spend the rest of that evening contemplating the difference between past and future, and my place stuck here smack-dab between the two. Our human artifacts, from stone tool to spent nuclear fuel rods, tell us who we have been. In the present time there are millions of humans who scramble over garbage heaps looking for food, while a handful of others bathe in riches. Ultimately, as science and human consciousness tells us, in the future there may be nothing left of humanity except the objects we leave behind. We owe it to the future of life on this planet to ensure that our artifacts do not threaten the possibility of existence.

I found the road into the yurt with no problem. We drove up the dusty path and parked where the windmill had stood. Now only its collapsed frame remained, the gray-bleached bones scattered about on the sunbaked yellow desert. There was no trace of the water tank.

We got out of the car, and I led the boys and Linda toward the site, following a path only I could see. It was as if I watched a film playing in my memory and simply followed it. But after a half mile or so, I lost confidence. I knew we were close, but where was the yurt? The four of us spread out and began to zigzag through the juniper and piñon, looking for any clue. Then Linda called out. She had found a metal frame of some sort. Once I joined her, it took me a moment to recognize that she had discovered the remains of the school desk that once served as my toilet in the outhouse.

Soon I found where the yurt had been. The floor was still there, although each pie piece had fallen off the foundation and was collapsed and rotting in a misshapen clutter. I recalled a stone step but saw instead a triangular rock jutting from the ground that seemed as familiar as family, and as strange. Any other trace of the yurt itself was gone. Either it had rotted away, or scavengers from Madrid had dismantled it.

I didn't generate a lot of debris at the yurt, I am proud to say. The plans were so well designed that there was virtually no wasted wood, and what little rubbish I had while I lived there I burned in a fifty-gallon drum. What didn't burn, including the fifty-gallon drum itself and some old food cans smashed by some unknown crush of wind or snow or hoof, had all but disappeared into a few small metal scraps rusting into nothingness on the desert ground, around them the sparkling false diamonds of shards of broken glass.

I began to move about the area, searching in the dust for the past.

What followed was the strangest forty-five minutes of my life, for I became an archeologist of my own history. From the artifacts left behind, I tried to better understand the man who had once lived here. I discovered a nail here, a scrap of wire there, the broken rim from an old coffee cup I recognized instantly.

What I had believed was my memory of those days confronted the reality of vague, ghostly artifacts scattered on the desert; true memory, like a body below the surface of a pool, tried to rise up with each found object.

15

_ _ _ _ _ _ _ _ _

Solitude

Although the intervening years have allowed me to romanticize the memories of living at the yurt, there is no denying the fact that I was never more alone than the time I spent there. A month would often pass without me seeing another human being. The solitary days marched by with my forced regime of habit and pattern, that therapeutic monotony broken only by occasional forays into the unexplored areas of the desert that surrounded me or by the rare visit from a friend.

Since the main purpose of my sojourn in the desert was to write, I sat nearly every morning at my manual typewriter and beat on the keys for an hour or two. Trusting the muse of inspiration, I let my fingers fly where they would. I wrote poems, letters, lists of supplies to buy, and short stories that left me cold the instant I finished them. As I said, nothing I wrote while living at the yurt was any good. If my goal for living there had been to become a writer, then by any stretch of the imagination, I failed.

Looking back at it, it seems odd to me that I would write so poorly, given the number of words I must have had pent up inside me. You would think, as I was bottled up there with nobody to talk to, my voice would go wild on the printed page. Not so, although I continued to try nearly every morning I was there.

When the day's frustrating writing session ended, I would push my chair away from my desk and walk out into the glare of the desert sun. Then, no matter what I did—work on the roof, fiddle with my meager plants, get water from the well, or simply roam the desert—I confronted only the unsoiled natural world. Like the ants, snakes, rodents, birds, and other creatures of the desert, I would hide in the shade from the midday sun and then go back out again, roaming and working until the stars danced about.

Aside from the dog, with whom I shared a good deal of my thoughts, there was no one to bounce my words off, to see if what I heard on the rebound sounded reasonably sane and cogent. Given that isolation, there wasn't much difference between what I spoke to the dog and what I thought without speaking. No matter what else, solitude forces you to confront fundamental questions of the self, to be faced with constant reminders of how thin the veneers of ego and self-image really are.

I was alone, but I was seldom lonely. Loneliness is different than solitude. Loneliness is being unhappy with yourself. Being caught up in doubt about your own worth, you can't imagine how anyone else could find something of value in you. Before long that kind of thinking descends into self-pity and self-loathing. Soon enough you find yourself in a different kind of isolation, a loneliness of the spirit, where you create elaborate charades of false confidence and emotional justifications in an attempt to get on in a world full of people who seem to want to have nothing to do with you.

It is possible to be lonely in the midst of a crowd, in the bosom of a family, or in a cabin in the desert. Loneliness is universal, but solitude is, well, solitary. It *requires* isolation. Thoreau said that once, shortly after coming to the woods at Walden Pond, he had felt lonesome "for an hour" and had started to think being alone was something unpleasant. "But I was at the same time conscious of a slight insanity in my mood." That insane mood passed when he began to contemplate the natural world all around him. He decided that "there can be no very black melancholy to him who lives in the midst of Nature and has his senses still."

For the most part we care only about the most trivial and transient things in our lives: our work, food, shopping, social obligations, gossip and rumors, television or internet or iPods, and phones. These distractions allow us to avoid contemplating the essential questions of existence. Just look into a starry night and consider the vast distances of time and space: by any kind of comparison, we are always close enough to a human neighbor. But seldom do we find in society anything more than a mindless unconcern with such infinite issues. We avoid confronting the essential facts of life by our texting, superficial chatter, and selfish blind desire to look good.

When we are distracted by society, we can't become aware of what Thoreau called our "spectator." No matter how intense an experience, Thoreau said he was aware of the presence of a spectator that doesn't share in the experience but simply takes note of it. This spectator is nothing more or less than our own mind. To truly live, to be mindful of our own consciousness, we need to look inside ourselves rather than outside at those people and things that surround us. Loneliness has nothing to do with the distances we are from one another but rather with how isolated we have become from self-awareness. Our days are crowded with people. Society is easy to find. The crowd of people and of things allows us to ignore the persistent yet faint presence of that spectator who reminds us of the infinity of time. Without solitude in our lives, away from the pollution of society, we will never be aware of this quality of consciousness.

Late in the afternoon, when the sun's heat was finally giving way to the coming dusk, I would set aside the enforced busyness of my day. I had built a small fire pit of stones not far from the yurt; and almost every evening, I would retire there to cook my meal and watch the night come on. I would sit before the crackling fire, its juniper-piñon perfume mixing with the sage-like smell that seems everywhere in desert country. From where I sat, the land slid down toward the distant Galesteo River amid craggy canyons and across vast plains. The wide, empty basin was the color of straw. Sixty miles beyond, the towering Sangre de Cristo Mountains turned the color of blood in the setting sun.

It was then that my thoughts had time to take root and unfold themselves. It was then that I most often missed the company of others—not the crowded-street-corner, busy-workplace kind of society, but the company of a friend or friends with whom I might share thoughts and laughter. When the vastness of the view beyond became too much, I sought the face of another human being seated close and comforting in the warm light of the fire.

Instead, the nighthawks appeared each night just before sunset, calling out in their high-pitched faint whistles and swooping down to grab insects from the cooling air. When they dove, their wings buzzed like cards shuffled by an unseen hand. When they appeared, I imitated their call so that soon they circled directly above me. Then I would throw a handful of dry dog food into the air and watch them plunge for it to within inches of where I sat.

Many nights, a family of coyotes traversed a nearby dry river arroyo. The dog would sense them first, and soon I could hear them too. Unconcerned, they would yip and cackle, bark and whine and yodel their way past me.

The coyotes were not anxious about tomorrow; the nighthawks never fretted over war or the price of fuel or petty gossip. Like them, I confronted nothing but the bare essentials of life: water, food, shelter. I did not understand it then, but living such a simple and pure life made me at peace with the world as it is. We become what we are: caught up in the rat race of life, trying to be the last voice heard, we become prideful and selfish. For that year of solitude in the wild desert, I was no more significant than the rocks and the dust. My life was but twilight on the wings of a nighthawk in a dark-turquoise sky.

My life at the yurt was a disciplined one. Although my writing was lousy and I never did get the roof absolutely leakproof, I kept myself busy. To waste away my days in lethargy would soon lead to madness—of this I was certain. And yet it was an idyllic life as well. I was so alone and in such closeness to the natural world that I came to exist in an easy, mindful harmony with it.

Although no houses are visible, here in Vermont my neighbors are close. I only have to walk a quarter mile to visit them. Vermont consistently ranks as the most rural state in the Union, which means that per capita more people live in the countryside than in any other state in the United States. That means that a lot of people live in these Vermont hills. Even in the most remote parts of the state, you are always within close proximity of other human beings.

Still, solitude and isolation are to be found here as well, for—as I said—loneliness has little to do with how close you are to another person.

I spent many hours alone working on the straw bale house. Instead of contemplative, productive solitude, this isolation brought loneliness and dissatisfaction. If it is true, as Diane Ackerman asserts, that what we pay most attention to transforms us, then during the time I built the straw bale house, I was changed from a human being to mechanical tool: my body a bucket full of nails, my soul a hammer ceaselessly pounding without emotion, all in service of this thing that had to be finished no matter what. The pressure of completing my house was changing me into someone I did not like, a detached automated creature, but one that I could not abandon.

If loneliness is being unhappy with the self, then I was never as lonely as I was during the long days while building the straw bale house. Even when surrounded by the helpful hands of the Amoeba, I was aware of my spirit's deep loneliness and of the farce of confidence I displayed. One of my friends commented how I was the only one who never lost his cool while building the house. What he never understood was that to lose my cool would be a wasteful extravagance of emotions, a self-indulgent divergence from the demands of what needed to be done.

The only reason this spiritual isolation did not finally ruin me was that I was able to recapture a tiny bit of the blessed solitude I once knew so perfectly long ago at the yurt. Ironically, I was able to salvage enough small shreds of my spirit in the nights I spent alone in a small trailer parked on a little knob just up from the house site.

We decided we could save a lot of time, gas, and money, if I had a place to sleep at the land while we built the house. We budgeted $2,000 for a used hard-shell camper, with the idea that we would sell it once we finished construction.

One day in spring, just weeks before we started building in earnest, we drove to a local sales lot. Too many idle men in nice shirts and slacks came out of the heated showroom and began to show us around. All but one guy drifted away once I convinced them that I wanted to see the cheapest camper on the lot.

The salesman glanced longingly at his retreating colleagues. "The cheapest on the lot? Well, we do have a 1987 fifth wheeler . . ." he said. "It came in here on a trade awhile back." He explained that a fifth wheeler is a trailer that hooks only into the bed of a pickup truck.

"We don't have a pickup," Linda whispered, as if to remind me.

He led us past Queen Elizabeth II—sized tour busses and large, shiny campers, to a short, plump metal box at the very back edge of the very far side of the very big lot.

We stepped inside. It was tiny but comforting. A toilet, sink, and shower were squeezed into a tiny room. There was a cozy loft that slept two, while at the far end there was a table and benches that collapsed into another bed. The stove worked, the fridge "probably works fine," and the gas heater . . . well, if we completed the exterior of the house on time, there would be no need for the heater anyway.

Before it even appeared at the house site, a friend had already christened it. The "Love Shack" was delivered a week later by a man in a large pickup truck, who drove up the snowy-edged drive-way to drop it off at the land. He made several tries, spinning tires on the icy soil before he was able to zigzag it to the ideal spot I had chosen for it at the top of the drive. We eventually got it in place, leveled and secured with small tripod jacks at each corner.

I gave the guy a tip for his gallant effort and watched him drive away. It was the end of March, and the sun was setting through the gray-blue branches of a cold late-winter sky. I waited until I could not hear his truck anymore, before I opened the door and stepped inside.

I had brought with me a huge stack of papers that absolutely had to be graded. I figured I wouldn't have much to distract me at the Love Shack. The late-winter dusk came early and stayed late. I cooked a simple meal on the stove and ate by candlelight. I crawled into the bunk and listened to a barred owl whoo-coo-coo-cooing. It took only that long for me to fall asleep.

The Love Shack soon became my home away from home and construction headquarters for building the house. Before long the unused bathroom became a shelter for tools and plumbing ma-terials and anything else I could fit. I kept the house plans on one of the benches so that I could spread them out on the small table. I kept a pot of coffee on the stove and a bottle of wine and some beer in a cooler, so that most every friend who helped us sooner or later found her or his way inside.

On one wall was a clock perpetually stuck at a few minutes past five. A running joke had it that no drinking was allowed until it was past five. So yes, a few glasses of wine and a cold beer or two were also always available at the Love Shack.

The calm solitude I found that first night in the Love Shack never vanished. No matter how frenzied the next eight months became, no matter how horrible the day had been, no matter what crisis loomed, and no matter how distant and cold my heart and soul had become, when I stepped inside that tiny space, I found a place of solitude and peace.

It seems incredible, but despite all the coldness in my heart and soul, every night I spent in the Love Shack was perfect. I had the deepest of sleeps and the gentlest of dreams. It was as if the thin walls of that rusting antique sheltered me from the loveless world outside and from the loveless one inside. Most nights during the coming months, I climbed inside the Love Shack, exhausted by the brutally tiring day, hounded by a million and one thoughts, and troubled by doubt. Instantly, once inside that intimate space, there was love and contentment. The nights of comfort there were as precious and rare a gift as life has ever brought me.

I would awake with the first hint of dawn, fire up some coffee, and listen to the birds come alive in the golden sunrise. I stepped outside to find the woods on fire with the deep green of high summer, the canopy of their crowns ablaze in the new light. Then in the awakening world of my solitary walk down the hill to the house, if only for one sanity-saving moment, I forgave myself and could begin again.

16

Visitors

One early evening at the yurt, I had just gathered firewood for my cooking fire when I stood dead still, listening. At first, there was nothing but the high, lonely whine of the desert insects, but then I heard it again. From far off on the highway the faint sound of a car horn honked with the pattern of our predetermined sign: SHAVE-AND-A-HAIRCUT . . . SHAM-POO.

"Wilson!" I shouted aloud, dropping my cooking pot to the ground. I grabbed the dog, threw her inside the yurt so she could not chase after me, and began running for the road. "Wilson!" I cried again.

Six weeks earlier my best friend from college, Jim Wilson, had written to tell me he was coming to New Mexico for a visit. He had an approximate idea of when he would come, and I gave him approximate directions on how to find me. I told him how to get to a certain point on the state highway that came nearest the yurt. Once he got there, he was to lay on the horn and wait until I came out to the road to direct him in. For days, I had been listening for the sound of his horn.

I started for the windmill at a run, but then I heard him honk again, fainter this time. He had driven farther away and was going too far down the highway. I started to sprint, picking my way around rocks and trees, too anxious about him and ignoring the time of day.

Politely the rattlesnake chose to slither away from me before it coiled and rattled. In that half instant, I had just enough time to stumble back and stop. The snake had been using the cool shadows of the early evening to hunt for food. It was a big one; the dust-colored pattern of diamonds on its back slowly undulated as it studied me. The string of pale-gray buttons on its tail rattled like dry bones shaken by some devil's hand.

I backed away and went around it in a wide circle. On any other evening, I would not have been running; on any other evening, I would have been on a keen lookout for snakes; on any other evening, I would likely have been carrying a walking stick or my shovel, using it to alert rattlers to my approach. But the thought of seeing my friend had distracted me.

I needn't have worried about Jim. Just as I reached the windmill, I saw the lights of his car bouncing toward me on the dusty path from the highway. The car wheezed to a stop. My old friend jumped out of the car. With his neat Vandyke beard and furrowed brow, he looked like a benevolent cross between Mark Twain and Charlie Manson.

Jim was about the best companion I could have. Like me, he had been an English major, and he could talk forever about books and ideas. In our final years at college our friendship had deepened during smoky barroom conversations and coffee-house debates over Faulkner and Hemmingway and whether someone would be able to stop Nixon's easy ride to a second term as president.

That night, sitting outside at the yurt, we talked for hours. We sat by the crackling fire, tossing our words into the rising smoke of its flames. We drank whiskey and listened to the coyotes' call. Soon enough the conversation came around to literature. I mentioned that the writer Jack Schaefer lived just up the road.

Fig. 11. James C. Wilson at the yurt, July 1973

Jim nearly jumped up. "You're kidding me," he said. "Jack Schaefer lives near here?"

Jack Schaefer's small novel *Shane* came out in 1949 but did not become widely known until the mid-1950s when a revised edition established the book as a classic in American literature. In the ice-cold cadence of simple declarative sentences, Schaefer tells the story of a lone drifter who appears at a homesteaders' house. "He rode into our valley in the summer of '89," the book begins, "a slim man, dressed in black."

"Call me Shane" is all the man would ever say about himself.

The emotional and psychological solitude of the stranger is so vivid that the reader chills at his isolation. Often mistaken as a kid's book about the Old West, *Shane* is instead a remarkable portrait of the possibility of human dignity in the face of deep, moral choices and the specter of the dark past.

Its author, Jack Schaefer lived on a ranch higher up in the Ortiz. He had moved there after the success of *Shane*. He was still writing books. In 1963, ten years before I built the yurt, he wrote the novel *Monte Walsh* while living at his ranch. The novel follows two close friends from youth to old age. They are cowboys, but the West is changing. The automobile is replacing the horse, and telephone lines dot the horizon. Eventually one of them moves to town and becomes a banker, but the other, Monte Walsh, refuses to give up the old pure ways of living.

The next day, Jim and I drove to the front gate of Jack Schaefer's ranch. A dirt road went beyond the gate and up into the Ortiz. In the far distance, we could make out the house itself. After a while we simply turned the car around and drove off. No, I never met him. I never had the courage to go up that long dusty road to his ranch, to knock on his door. What was I to tell him? That I lived alone like a hermit but that I loved his books? That I loved how he could take the very soil itself and turn that red-and-yellow powder into dreams?

Thanks to Jim's visit, for the next several days, I rejoined the human race. For a week, we talked, hiked, and went sightseeing. We joked and we drank. We played cards, visited Santa Fe, drove aimlessly around the area, and laughed.

I had a few other visitors that year. My mother came, a brother or two, Bob and Jim from Cornucopia, and the regular visits from Brenda. Even Henry Thoreau said that he was not naturally a hermit and that if the prospect of a good conversation was at hand, he could "sit out the sturdiest frequenter of the bar-room."

Unlike Thoreau, I didn't always have much patience with the numerous visitors we got while we were building our straw bale house. Often times a car would slowly make its way down the driveway. A quick glance told us they were strangers who had heard about our project. "Tourists," we began to call them. Work would slow as either Linda or I showed them around. People were curious to see what we were doing. Some came just to see how a house made of straw looked, others had simply heard about it and showed up, while still others came to find out more about sustainable living.

Perhaps the most interesting were the handful of visitors who came because they were going to be building their own straw house and wanted to study what we were doing. These included a visit from a polite couple who were just starting the process of building a small, sustainable house. They asked great questions about the design of our house and listened closely as I explained the financial complications of our decision to go off grid.

Another woman visited because her daughter was about to start construction of a straw bale house and wanted to learn how to do it so that she could help her daughter. She showed up one day with two coolers full of ice and drinks and said she had come to help. She had heard that it is possible to do a lot of the building with the help of friends. We had never met her before. We were pouring the concrete floor that day. I was trying to direct the parade of huge cement trucks trying to back their way down the drive. Linda thanked her and gave her back the coolers.

Then there was the man from New York City. He had contacted me via e-mail. A friend of a friend of a friend had told him about us. He had recently bought a few acres in upstate New York and was planning on building a sustainable house. He asked if he could stop by on his next trip north. He was particularly interested in learning about how straw bale was done. We picked a date via e-mail when I knew we would be in the midst of putting in the straw.

On the appointed day, he showed up—a neatly dressed, quiet man in his early forties. We shook hands and talked briefly, but then the work day began. Throughout the day of organized chaos—replete with everything from completing an entire wall to the crisis of a broken tool—he studied what was happening. He never got in anyone's way but inspected everything carefully. He took notes on a small pad he kept in his shirt pocket, and occasionally asked if he could snap a photograph. He was remarkably involved in everything we did that day and remarkably nonintrusive. He asked if he could climb up ladders and then did so only when it was clear no one needed it at that moment. Once on top he squeezed into the tightest of places to get a better look at, say, how you need to insulate the place where the straw meets the roofline. He stayed until midafternoon. Before he left, he came to say good-bye. He waited until I was not busy, chatted a moment, shook my hand again, and was gone.

If we spend time like money, then that visitor was a rich man. He did not waste my time, and he certainly did not waste his own. He never stopped paying attention to what we were doing. Once he had absorbed as much as he thought he could get, he left.

Thoreau got a lot of "tourists" at Walden too. He claimed that over twenty were packed into his tiny cabin once. He had three chairs at his cabin: one for himself, the second for a friend, and the third for society. Thoreau was generous with his time. He knew that many of his visitors would never come again. He understood too that communicating with others always involves a risk.

Visitors come and go, the result of chance. Sometimes they appear out of nowhere like ghosts on the wispy edge of our life and then disappear. Other times they appear with the car horn blaring and endure as lifelong friends. But if we are indifferent at the appearance of a visitor, then we are indifferent to being alive. They may welcome us or shun us, but if we do not give up our own isolation and try to understand those around us, society itself will not endure.

17

- - - - - - - - -

Thick Skin in a Winter of Discontent

I. The First Coat

By late summer in the year we built our straw bale house, the real estate crisis was in full force. No one was interested in buying our Victorian house. In fact there had only been three or four people who had viewed the place all summer long. One said it was too small. (Small? The house had three or four bedrooms, an office, and a formal dining room! It had enough space to raise an army.) Another told the Realtor that they didn't like the neighborhood. (*Neighborhood?* In a town of less than six thousand?)

On September 11 six years after the national tragedy, Linda spoke with the bank about our predicament. Our plan had been to turn our expensive construction loan into a mortgage as soon as we sold our Victorian; but since nothing anywhere was selling, we were making payments on both the loan and our old mortgage. We would go broke if we had to do that for very much longer.

There was not much the bank could do about it, except to extend our construction loan for another year. That, at least, bought me a little more time to complete the construction. We tried not to panic, but the darkness seemed ominous. Winter was coming. No houses were selling anywhere, and more than half the work on the straw bale had yet to be done. On top of everything else, the family dog—the easygoing mutt that had survived the boys' teenage years—was dying. She had internal bleeding due to a growth on her spleen, as well as severe arthritis in her spine. At night we awoke to her howls of pain; and in the morning, we found that she could barely stand. It grew so bad that we knew we had to end her suffering.

The day our veterinarian came to put her down, I had to be at the construction site early. Andy and Daniel were coming back to plaster. Before first light I said my good-byes to the dog, by lying on the floor next to her snout. She twitched; and although her eyes were glazed, she stared at me and then sighed. Both of our grown sons were in town that day and were able to say farewell to their old pet. Linda bore the brunt of it, having to sit with her until the vet's injection did its duty and our old pet was gone. Linda and our sons decided to have her cremated.

If a person needs to grieve for a family pet, then I missed that requirement. I had the stress of the next big step in building our house. I had everything Andy and Daniel had ordered me to have ready; I had rented a giant compressor, stockpiled bags of lime, ordered truckloads of sand, and covered all the windows and doors with tarps.

The plaster covering of a straw bale house functions as its skin. It protects the bales from rain and snow as well as from interior moisture. It also reinforces the building against high winds or earthquakes. In addition, it adds beauty to the finished structure. Most importantly, the plaster covering helps to allow the straw to breathe—that is, to allow water vapor to escape to the outside. Because cement does not allow vapor to pass, few straw bale houses are plastered in concrete. If they are, the bales are sealed in and often deteriorate. As a result, most straw bale builders use a plaster made from clay, sand, lime, and a binder like chopped straw. At least three different coats of plaster are applied in order to cre-

Fig. 12. Daniel applying the first coat of stucco .

ate a thick layer of protection. Each coat uses a different sand size. The idea is to use coarse sand in the first, finer sand in the second, and only lime in the third coat. Water vapor will wick its way out from the straw, finding its way through the largest sand particles first, while on the exterior wall, because of the small diameter of the lime particles, water from rain and snow will tend to bead up and shed away. When finished, a plastered straw bale wall is not only beautiful, but it also serves as the final surface of a very efficient thermal barrier.

A big advantage of building with straw is its ability to insulate. How well a material resists heat flow from one side to the other is called its R-value: the higher the R-value, the better the insulation. The R-value of a typical modern house is about R-18. The walls of a typical straw house are R-49. The difference is like spending a cold winter's night wrapped in a heavy quilt rather than a thin sheet.

In addition, the R-value for the roof insulation is very important. "When it comes to the insulation in your roof," one of my advisors told me, "make like Babe Ruth and go deep." So I spent several days blowing cellulose insulation into our attic before I reached a thickness that gave me about R-90. A standard house is often less than R-30. While I used a common commercial insulation— blown-in cellulose made from recycled fibrous materials—there are even more sustainable options. Although you have to build extra-strong walls and take many precautions against fire, straw bales have been used as roof insulation. Other natural insulation includes a product called Air Krete, which is made from minerals and sea water. One of the most interesting ways to insulate your roof is to use raw wool. I learned that one from Daniel, who told me he insulated his roof with wool he got for free from various Massachusetts woolen mills, who gladly gave him their scraps.

II. The Second Coat

On a Monday in late October, Daniel and Andrew returned for the three-day-long job of applying the second coat of plaster. Daniel arrived first, driving down to the house in his hamburger-and-fries-smelling biodiesel truck. A stout, strong-framed man in his late thirties, he jumped out and greeted me. Ten minutes later Andy arrived, pulling a flatbed trailer loaded with the blower and other equipment we would need. Andy emerged, all seriousness behind a furrowed brow.

We went inside and inspected the work I had done in the two months since we had built the straw walls. Everything was ready. The interior ceiling was finished; it had been a nightmare of a job. A wall made of straw has no even edges like a wall of Sheetrock and lumber. Instead of a nice straight line, the junction where the straw meets the ceiling is undulating and wavy. That means I had to custom cut each sheet of Sheetrock (our ceiling is about the only place we used Sheetrock in the house). While such lines give the interior walls of a straw bale house its organic beauty, matching them up with the flatness of a ceiling was a cumbersome and difficult job. Instead of simply securing the Sheetrock in place, I had to raise each heavy sheet to the ceiling, mark it against the curvy shape of the wall, lower it, cut the Sheetrock along the line, and then repeat the process a half dozen times until the cut was perfect.

"That looks good," Andy said. "And you have the sand all ready?"

We moved back outside and set to work. We unloaded the trailer, set up a staging platform for the mixer, ran power lines (by then my solar power system was up and running), got the water hose in place, and began.

The second coat of plaster for my walls was made from lime, sand, and water. My job was to keep Daniel supplied with the raw materials. I filled five-gallon buckets with sand I got from a big pile at the side of the drive. I carried bucket after bucket to Daniel, who hoisted them and dumped them into a large, electrically powered mixer. I also opened eighty-pound bags of lime, and together we wrestled them into the churning blades of the mixer. Daniel sprayed it all down with just the right amount of water. Once a batch was finished, we dumped it into a large wooden hopper. From the hopper, we fed the raw stucco into the blower, which pushed it through a thick undulating tube to the inside of the house, where Andy, speckled head to toe in gray plaster, sprayed it onto the walls.

Despite my confidence that Andy and Daniel would laugh at the idea, Linda made sure I took the metal box containing the ashes of our dog with me one morning during their stay.

"Of course!" they both shouted, nearly in unison. "Of course you can add her ashes to the mix!" They told me I wasn't the first person who had included a family pet's ashes in the stucco of a house.

They stood while I opened the box and lifted out the plastic package. Whoever had cremated her had put her ashes inside double plastic bags—the large kind with the ziplock seal. I stood over the big mixer and removed the interior bag. It was surprisingly heavy, for a dog that weighed less than thirty pounds when alive. I pried open the bag and held it against the lip of the mixer. I stood it upright and watched the dark-charcoal flecks swirl into the gray. Then Daniel and I tipped the mixer, and the new plaster fell into the hopper. Andy nodded, picked up the spraying tube, and resumed his work too.

If I felt anything, it was only a kind of astonishment at my own insensitivity. My faithful pet's death seemed to mean nothing to me. I knew I should feel something—*wanted* to feel something for the poor dog and for the way her passing affected my family; but all I felt was more of the numbness that had been with me since long before we ever started construction.

Earth-based plasters have been used all over the world for centuries. The oldest houses in the United States—the ancient adobe pueblos of New Mexico—have been covered in such plasters for centuries. Modern-day adobe houses are still plastered with essentially the same materials that have been used for over a thousand years.

I had hitchhiked down from the yurt to Cornucopia the day they replastered the old adobe that served as the main building for the commune. I caught a ride all the way with an ancient Hispanic man who was headed to see his cousin somewhere near La Bajada, the big hill halfway between Albuquerque and Santa Fe. He dropped me off at the mailbox around midmorning.

Several people were already at work. Everyone from the commune was there, plus an artist I had met before. Jim Exten painted exquisitely imaginative renderings of bones and feathers or quirky human portraits bordered by a dancing line of raven-beaked figures. Idiosyncratic in his keen observations, handsome, and strong—Jim was an ideal companion. Like me, he had wandered into the circle of expanding friends that was centered at Cornucopia. He knew a little about plastering and had volunteered to help. When I arrived, he had just started.

I picked up a trowel and tried to catch on to what he was doing. "Where do I begin?" I asked.

"That's good," he said to me, nodding at the trowel. "But you'll need a hawk, too." He handed me what appeared to be an eight-inch square piece of plywood with a wooden handle on one side. "The hawk is where you pile a working load of plaster," he said. He led me to a wooden trough filled with plaster. Other people were adding materials to a second trough and mixing the plaster with long, narrow-handled hoes.

I glopped a bunch of the plaster onto my plywood hawk. It had the consistency and color of chocolate ice cream that had melted just enough to scoop easily into a dish. I followed Jim back to the house and watched him begin.

"You need to make sure there is a little moisture on the adobe so the plaster will stick to it," he said. He held the edge of the hawk against the wall where several new but exposed adobe bricks had replaced older ones. He used his large rectangular trowel and slid a bit of the plaster until it covered a small section of the exposed adobe bricks.

"You want to work it in with a bit of pressure; make sure that it is going to stick," he said. He was a year or two younger than I was and—to my way of thinking—far more creative. I watched him work more plaster onto the wall. Soon he began to sweep his trowel across the wet plaster in long, graceful arcs until it shimmered as if glass. Instead of a trowel, it was as if he held a paintbrush, and that old wall was his canvas.

It was not so simple when I tried. While Jim's artistic sensitivity and attention to detail served him well, I worked much slower and with far less satisfying results. Sometimes the plaster would fall off the wall as soon as I put it there. My work with the trowel left unsightly lines where the steel edge had cut deeply into the fresh muddy surface.

I switched from the finish work to helping mix the plaster. I carried buckets of sand, shoveled in clay, and dumped bags of lime into the trough. We poured in ox blood to color the plaster and shoveled manure in to bind it.

We stopped working and had a big lunch; there were sandwiches on thick homemade bread, fruit, and gallons of ice tea. A radio played. People talked and laughed. We set to work again in no particular hurry, and by late afternoon we were finished. The old adobe house glimmered in the golden sunlight; the wet, smooth plaster, the color of the earthen hills that surrounded us.

We found our way inside and soon had plates heaped with summer stew made of squash and tomatoes, carrots and kale. We ate more of that great bread and washed everything down with goblets of red wine. After the dishes got washed and things were put away, we sat down in the big common room, passed the jug of wine, and let the conversation flow.

Cornucopia almost had it right, almost had regained that lost knowledge of interdependence. But no pastoral community can survive simply by hoping and believing in the possibility of human harmony.

The fire that destroyed the community known as Cornucopia was two weeks later.

The blind, romantic idealism that created Cornucopia was responsible for far more tragic failures. Vermont's Earth People's Park, Wavy Gravy's dream of "free land for free people," ended in crime, squalor, and greed. Even many communities that formed because of a religious vision—especially those communes—produced not a more harmonious world but a more evil and darker one.

Linda and I were living in Oregon in 1981 when a large religious commune appeared almost overnight in the central part of the state. Soon the commune had taken over an entire county. Before long their exploits were being reported nationwide.

The commune's residents were followers of Bhagwan Shree Rajneesh, a self-proclaimed Indian guru who combined classic philosophy, mysticism, and other religious traditions to create a vision of spiritual perfection. Among other surprising tenants, his teachings included euthanasia for children born with birth defects and the use of genetic selection to improve humanity.

In June 1981, following mounting tensions with the Indian government, Rajneesh fled his commune in Poona, India. In July his followers purchased a 64,000-acre ranch in Oregon, claiming they were going to start "a simple farming community" with about fifty people. Within months, over two hundred people lived at Rajneeshpuram, as the commune was soon named. The following year enough Rajneeshees had moved to the area that they successfully took over the city council of Antelope, Oregon. They immediately called for a vote and changed the name of the town to Rajneesh. Once in power, they created their own police force, and many of the original residents of the area were harassed. Soon the Rajneeshees began busing hundreds of street people from around the United States to the commune in an effort to have the votes needed to control the countywide elections. Then, a county executive who visited the commune nearly died of poisoning. Doctors discovered "a highly toxic substance" in his kidneys.

Six weeks before the November 1984 elections, leaders of the commune made the first bioterror attack in U.S. history. Afraid that they still did not have enough votes to win control of Wasco County, followers of Rajneesh decided they would incapacitate voters in the county's most populous city, The Dalles. As a trial run for this plan, they contaminated the salad bars of ten local restaurants with salmonella. Over eight hundred people were sickened—many had to be hospitalized. It wasn't until nearly a year later, when Rajneesh himself accused his aids of the crime, that it became clear what happened. Later, informants claimed that the poisoning was just a test for a far more wide-reaching attack that had been planned to take place immediately before the elections in November. In addition, Rajneesh accused his aids of other crimes. People under the influence of his ideas tried to murder doctors, dentists, the Jefferson County district attorney, a Wasco County executive, a U.S. attorney, and Oregon attorney general David Frohnmeyer. They burned down a Wasco County government building, and they had plans to blow up the Wasco County Courthouse.

Although he claimed no part in these events, in 1985 Rajneesh pleaded guilty to two of thirty-five immigration charges pending against him. His plea bargain included deportation. He returned to India, changed his name to Osho, and created a new spiritual community known as the Osho International Meditation Retreat. He died in 1990. His ideas survive via a growing number of followers.

The darker side of human intent can also be found in far less notorious cases.

Almost any way you look at it, the school of *Las Tres Villas*, where I taught in Tesuque, was a success. A group of very diverse parents and others were able to create a good, viable school and to keep it running for an entire school year. Despite many times when tempers flared and anger threatened to ruin everything, the community survived and triumphed. We all thought that with our harmonious and successful work, we had changed something for the better. Maybe we had in some small way, but darkness too lurked just below the surface, even in those heady times.

Several days a week, I volunteered to drive the school bus. After a particularly exhausting Friday, I was driving the bus down the dead-end road where the last kid on the bus—we'll call him Eddie—was about to get off.

Earlier that day, Eddie had refused to stop bugging another student, and I sent him to the principal. He came back to class angry and sullen. Now I studied him in the rearview mirror. He glared at me from his seat.

I stopped at his home and opened the door. "See you next week," I said. He paused for only an instant. He muttered "*joto*" loud enough for me to hear and then stepped off the bus. He disappeared into his house.

I turned the school bus around in the narrow road and started to drive away. Just after I passed by his house, I looked in my rearview mirror to see him step onto the road, carrying a rifle. I floored it. Just before I ducked, I saw him lower the rifle and aim.

I don't think he fired any shots.

I spent the weekend thinking about what happened. How could an eleven-year-old feel such rage that he would threaten to kill me? What flaw in my own hubris about being a "teacher" had prevented me from helping him ease that anger? Would Eddie and the tens of thousands like him ever learn the sanctity of a human life?

On Monday morning Eddie greeted me as if nothing had ever happened. And nothing more ever did. Although he continued to get in trouble now and then for the rest of the year, he was never again as angry at me as he had been that day. Yet the incident haunts me still, for it demonstrated the inherent danger in believing that a collective movement, by its common goals and righteousness, gains immunity to the darkest aspects of human interaction.

Take, for example, the community revival of Madrid, New Mexico. Today that history is told with pride by the boosters of the area and justly so. However, not all the people who originally reoccupied the village lived the hippie ideals of peace, love, and understanding. Because I was so isolated, I never had any trouble from my fellow human beings when I lived at the yurt; but by the time I moved away from there, Madrid's big boom was beginning, bringing a wide assortment of humanity to the area. About a year after I moved out, I visited the yurt to discover that someone had stolen my woodstove.

The stove was one of the best, an Ashley. Despite the thin insulation on the yurt (the walls were probably less than R-5), a couple of juniper branches tossed into the belly of the Ashley would keep me warm an entire winter's night. The worse part about it was that the stove was not mine but on loan from Bob, the friend from Cornucopia who had given me the plans for the yurt. In any event, it was gone. Pack rats had found their way in through the stovepipe, and the place now had the sickly, chlorine-flavored smell of rodent urine.

Swept along on a tide about which I was then entirely ignorant, I first moved to New Mexico, and ultimately to the yurt, following a dream—fueled by books and ideas of self-determination and personal freedom. It was not just "every hippie's dream" but the waning of the great American dream—a dream of wealth and possibility set in a land of endless horizons. I was born on the great open plains of Nebraska at the start of the postwar prosperity of the 1950s. When I was a child, there were still old men and women in my town who had come west in covered wagons, following that old dream. By then their very lives were being transformed into myth in books like *Shane* and *Monte Walsh* and in the ubiquitous western cinema. When I left home, I wanted to find that Old Empty West, an infinite open wilderness to constantly humble, frighten, and inspire me. What I didn't know, or blithely ignored, was that the landscape of the yurt was but a tiny, quickly evaporating remnant of a world where limitless horizons seemed possible. Even that remnant was about to vanish: the new residents of Madrid had found the yurt, and the entire American Southwest was about to tremble under the stampede of millions of additional new immigrants—which has not yet abated. At the yurt, I witnessed a last fragment of what humankind had always taken for granted: a limitless earth, while even my own solitary intrusion was itself heralding its demise.

Flash forward to 2007 and our winter of discontent. The day Andy, Daniel, and I were embedding our dog's ashes into the second coat of plaster at the straw bale, Ameriquest, one of the largest subprime lenders in the United States, went out of business. In the following weeks home mortgage companies began to fall apart faster than the big bad wolf could blow down a house made of sticks. Before the first snows fell, we took the Victorian house off the market. Even in the best of times, few houses sold in winter; now with the Federal Reserve scrambling to prevent a crisis in the banking system, the housing market collapsed. Only Linda, bless her ever-hopeful heart, held onto the pale idea that we might still be able to sell the house ourselves.

As the days shortened and the nights turned colder, I burrowed myself deeper into the detached and soulless man I had become. My marriage dwindled down to days of stress and tensions, and nights of monosyllabic conversations sprinkled with tears and anger. The tenderest moments, if they could be called that, were the times I apologized to Linda for my incompetence, trying to explain that this big mess was all my fault, that she had married a man whose ego had always outreached his skills, only this time it might well destroy our future together.

Classes had started in September, giving me far less time to work on the house. While the straw bale house was now enclosed with doors and windows, the inside was nothing but a large, empty space. There were no interior walls, giving the vacuous room a forlorn and lonely feel. After teaching, I would race to the building site to work for hours until dark and exhaustion overcame me. As the weeks trudged on, I cut and measured and swore and hammered and cried. Little by little the skeletal insides of the house began to take the vague shape of walls and rooms.

In late October the Amoeba helped me install our woodstove. One night in early November when the temperature reached nineteen degrees, I abandoned the Love Shack for good and moved my bedding to the house. During the day, I piled my blankets in a corner. At night I slept on them on the floor in front of the fire, surrounded by tools, papers to be graded, bags of lime, wiring, lecture notes for my classes, plumbing, cabinets waiting to be installed, and stacks of thin pine boards for the walls.

The walls of the rooms inside the straw bale are pine tongue-and-groove boards rather than standard walls of Sheetrock. Building a green house meant looking at more-sustainable alternatives for everything. The pine walls didn't need to be painted, and we found the bright but rustic look of the natural wood attractive. The use of wood for our walls also meant we could buy a product that was manufactured close by (the wood came from Quebec, just north of Vermont) and that took fewer resources to manufacture and transport.

The stacks of boards competed for space with one large crate about the size of a piano bench. The crate held a heat-recovery ventilator (an HRV), the device that would circulate fresh air in my airtight house. The HRV was going to be put in a hidden compartment above a small coat closet.

On a dark winter's day, I stood on a small ladder, preparing to install the HRV. The crate was just below me. I leaned into the compartment, and then . . . I fell.

I landed on the sharp corner of the crate. The full force of it hit my ribcage like the blow of an ax.

It had been a long while since I wept out of shear pain. For a very long while, I did not move. I tried to assess the pain, to coolly calculate the extent of my injury. Convinced that I had broken

Fig. 13. The author plastering the interior

several ribs and perhaps punctured a lung, I tried to calm myself. I was alone in the house; it was a weekday. There wasn't a phone of any kind. Finally, I moved, testing each inch against the amount of agony. I made my way over to a lawn chair, my only furniture, and sat down. I convinced myself that I had not broken any ribs, but I could not move without intense pain. I sat in the chair for the rest of the afternoon, before I drove back to the old house to spend the night with Linda. I didn't tell her about the incident until several days later.

III. The Final Coat

Linda kept a log of our adventure. She starts her brief account of the day we began to apply the final coat of plastering with two words: ANDREW'S EYES!

The final coat that covers our straw bale walls is a mixture of lime and water. Lime, which comes in large eighty-pound bags, is made by burning limestone in kilns. It is caustic and can burn the skin and eyes.

To make a lime wash, as this final coat is called, you mix lime in a large bucket with just enough water so that it has the consistency of whole milk. You can add color to it, as we did to our outside walls, or leave it white, as we did on the interior. The good thing about a lime wash is that it goes on quickly. You can slop it on with a wide brush in long strokes. It looks horribly streaky at first, but it dries to a beautiful pastel hue.

The day we started lime washing the inside walls, our son Andrew was home on a visit from college. Linda and he worked together putting the wash on the bathrooms, and then they joined me where I was working in the large common room.

I dipped my brush in the big bucket and wiped it on the wall near a window. Andrew worked next to me. He was standing to my left when he dropped his brush. "I got some in my eyes," he said. Then: "It hurts. It really hurts."

In that instant, everything turned to insanity—insanity, my plan to build such a house; insanity, not insisting he wear safety goggles; and insanity, my every single dream.

Later Linda would comment about how calm and cool I was. She said I calmed Andrew down by not panicking. I immediately began to flush his eyes with water. I told her to call the hospital and tell them what happened. Once we were in the emergency room, they put small contact lens—like devices in each of Andrew's eyes.

These were attached to bags of saline solution, one for each eye. They told him the lime was eating the protein in his eyes. He sat there for hours, until slowly the pH level of his eyes approached normal. The next day, an eye doctor said that his eyes were going to be okay and that if I hadn't acted so quickly, he would be blind.

That night, I lay in front of the woodstove. Surrounded by all the debris of an unfinished house, I cried and I cried and I cried.

18

Spring

Now and again, it is necessary to seclude yourself among deep
mountains and hidden valleys to restore your link to the source of life.

MORIHEI UESHIBA, *The Art of Peace*

The snowfall that winter was heavy—like the old days, the old-
time Vermonters said—but as the drifts grew deeper around our
door, the inside of our house looked more and more like a home.
We finished the interior walls, installed doors, put in kitchen
cabinets and bathroom sinks; we hooked up the telephone, attached the water heater, and hung light fixtures. Outside, the
world was a white mist of snow; nearby trees, dark skeletons
amid the haze. Snow slid off the metal roof in great thundering
rumbles, while inside, a toasty fire and the thick blanket of straw
kept me warm. Without fail, after each nor'easter, our neighbor
arrived in his big truck to plow out the drive. The temperature
dropped lower and lower until one night in late February, when
it reached twenty-six below zero. The next day, it never got above
zero. But the sun shone in a crystalline, cloudless sky, and the
drifts of snow glistened translucent and luminous. On that sunny, bitterly cold day, the sunlight filled the great room with its
warmth and gold.

Slowly, in the nearly imperceptible way of the seasons of a year
or a life, the dark and oppressive winter was becoming spring. One
morning just after first light, I awoke from my cocoon on the floor
in front of the woodstove, vaguely aware of another presence. I

stood up; and there, immediately outside the big glass windows, standing so close that I could count its eyelashes, was a white-tailed deer. It held its head as if listening and looking, now also aware it was not alone. The darkness of the inside of the house hid me. After an anxious moment, it lowered its head once again, allowing me to step even closer to the window.

The heat of the sun along the southern side of the house had melted the snow enough to expose a thin strip of ground. There, with winter apparently still in full power, the first sign of spring had appeared: a thin, gorgeous green thread of newly sprouted clover. The deer was pressed against the house, munching on the new forage. The long winter had been hard on the poor thing; its shaggy coat could not conceal the sharp outline of ribs and backbone. The head jerked up, its eyes level with mine, dark and moist and alive. Just an instant's glance, then it was gone. Bounding over a drift, over a small hill, it disappeared into the woods.

For perhaps the first time since we started building, I did not do any work that morning. Instead, I bundled up, strapped on a pair of snowshoes, and, telling myself I was simply curious to see where the deer had gone and would return shortly, set off into the woods. I spent hours just walking the hills of Vermont, stopping to look up through the bare branches of trees or to study the way a leaf had been caught, midtumble, in a drift of snow. I had no plan, no ambition, and no other place to be than right here.

I realized that morning how much of myself had been lost. For nearly two years, I had been so fixated on the need to get the house built that I had silenced that spectator within; I was no longer mindful of my own consciousness, to say nothing of my *conscience*. I had abandoned any contemplation of the here and now in exchange for what was next: next to be done, next on the list, the next obstacle; and if the heart, the body, or the mind got in the way, I simply made some heedless and temporary maneuver in order to relieve or ignore or escape the strain, before turning my attention back on the house.

For the length of that morning in those solitary, cold woods, I regained a little bit of my sanity. Perhaps the fog of callous indifference had finally started to lift. What I had been paying total attention to had defined me; it was time I sought a redefinition.

While I was the primary builder, Linda was the primary accountant. It had largely been her responsibility to keep the books for the project and to try to sell the Victorian house. Her anxiety over the prospect of our financial ruin easily matched my anxiety over building. But suddenly with spring came hope. A newly hired professor and his wife had heard we had been trying to sell our house, and they wondered if it were still available.

That weekend, the couple came over to our Victorian house with their two children to look it over. We greeted them and then left them alone in the house. "Feel free to snoop anywhere you want," we told them. "Open doors, climb into the attic, whatever you wish."

For the next ninety minutes, Linda and I drove around, nervously talking about this unexpected showing of our house. Since we had taken it off the market, we had used word of mouth (always effective in a small town) to let people know it was still available. Although most of the town knew it was for sale, these were the first people to take an interest.

When we walked back into the house, the two of them were talking about how they might use a spare room.

"She wants it for a kid's playroom," he said.

The woman threw up her arms. "And he wants to use it to store all his records and CDs!"

They were arguing over how to use the room. A good sign, I thought. I shot Linda a quick look, and she nodded, smiling.

A week later, after they returned for another look, they told us they wanted to buy the house. The four of us stood in our old kitchen talking. We negotiated. In turn, each couple crowded into the bathroom in order to discuss offers and counteroffers in private. Twenty minutes later we had a deal. We shook hands all around and then sat at the kitchen table and filled out the paperwork.

That night, we celebrated with friends. No matter what happened with the straw bale, we were no longer going to be paying for two houses. A week after we sold the house, the fifth-largest bank in the United States, Bear Stearns, folded because of its involvement in the real estate market. Investors no longer believed the bank could repay its loans.

Selling the house meant that Linda would be temporarily homeless. While I was comfortable sleeping on my mat on the floor in a dusty, still-under-construction house, it wouldn't do for her. The plumbing wasn't finished, so there was no running water. And there was no real living space for her. Soon enough, however, our problem was solved. Linda was to move into a spare bedroom thanks to—what else?—the Amoeba.

I left the yurt for as good a reason as I went there. The rest of my life called to me; my life there was not productive; I needed to make some money; I was bored; and I grew tired of checking for black widow spiders every time I sat down on that school-desk toilet.

What do I have to show for that time? Late in his masterpiece *A Hundred Years of Solitude*, Gabriel Garcia Marquez writes that a woman spent her final years "in the solitude of nostalgia." Is that all my experience comes down to: dreamlike walks down a sun-bright desert path in a memory of spring?

The artifacts of my time on the desert, the few scattered remnants that still endure at the site, will soon disappear back into the earth. Had that time been nothing more than an attempt to leave my mark on the earth? Why else do I write about it now? Isn't almost everything I have done in this life little more than wanting something of myself to endure: teaching, children, writing books, the yurt, this straw house? Perhaps our desire to leave something behind after we are gone will be humanity's ultimate downfall, for many of our human artifacts have spoiled the earth and will poison it long after we disappear.

And yet I look back on that year at the yurt not with nostalgia or despair but with hope that we shall withstand the changes that come, for I know that even an innocent, young, and ignorant man can live simply on the earth and find in that life deep self-reflection and human compassion.

The ancient pueblo-dwelling people of the Southwest, the Anasazi, often simply abandoned their cities. No one knows why they did so, but some archeologists believe it was because they were in constant search of a spiritual center—a place where the earth and heaven were connected. The ruins of their quest lie scattered everywhere across the desert Southwest. Perhaps the shards of broken glass, rotting wood, and twelve stone pillars of the foundation for a long-vanished yurt are nothing more or less than my own search for that center.

The day we moved into the straw bale house was also the largest single gathering of the Amoeba during the entire project: trucks and cars, boxes and moving vans, donuts and pots of black coffee, laughter and hard work. Men and women were all in motion.

I drove out with the first convoy of items being moved from the old house to the new.

The straw bale house was not finished. The master bedroom was barely more than a shell, and I was using the space as a workshop. I had moved the table saw, workbenches, unused lumber and hardware, as well as all my tools into the place where Linda and I were supposed to sleep. As load after load of a lifetime of possessions began to arrive, I directed my friends to stack things in one of the small bedrooms. When it was full, they piled things in the other small bedroom, until finally the old house was empty and the new was a cluttered chaos of our life. Since we didn't have space to set up the bed, I slept on the floor that night, and Linda on the couch.

The next day, the two of us returned alone to our old house, now empty save for the memories: our first night twenty years ago unpacking boxes and laughing while the children slept. The numberless holidays, the countless guests, the tears, and the deep comfort all passed in the twinkling of an eye.

"Living is the constant adjustment of thought to life and life to thought in such a way that we are always growing, always experiencing new things in the old and old things in the new," wrote Thomas Merton in *Thoughts in Solitude*. "Thus life is always new."

19

– – – – – – – – –

Higher Laws

1. *Sustainability* means to sustain the life of the entire planet for the time *after* we are gone.
2. Be aware of the environmental and the moral consequences of every personal action.
3. War and hatred are not sustainable.
4. Common interest comes before self-interest.
5. Try to make present circumstances better before building something new.
6. Study patterns that make things accessible, healthy, efficient, and sustainable and then replicate those patterns.
7. Keep it simple; simplicity gives an object its beauty.
8. Go lightly on the earth; use as little as possible.
9. Everything is in the act of becoming; nothing stays the same.

1. Sustainability

You can't escape the idea of sustainability—it is everywhere in modern culture. The problem is that the popular and commercial use of the word seems to mean nothing more than a new way to sell and consume goods. Everything is "green": from toilet paper to automobiles, from shampoo to kiddie toys, from junk food to appliances. Big business continues to prosper and consume resources under the illusion that it is sustaining the earth's resources; instead, it is creating a society even more dependent on "improved" consumer products.

The popular concept of sustainability does not address how resources are protected, much less distributed; and it promotes the very values that got us into trouble in the first place. Sustainability isn't simply about using the right lightbulb, buying "green" products, recycling, or even building an ecologically sensitive house. The real issue facing humankind is sustaining complicated, interwoven biotic communities, not sustaining a comfortable lifestyle for the privileged classes.

Sustainability is most commonly thought of in economic terms: making and consuming goods while being sensitive to the capacity of the earth's resources. The goal seems to be to keep modernization alive and well. Many environmentalists abhor such attitudes. For many, the common concept of sustainability fails to acknowledge the need for drastic changes in how we humans live.

Just before we took the plunge and began construction, Linda and I had a long and frank talk about what such a house might mean to the way we lived our life. There would have to be changes in our habits: we'd have to become misers in our use of electricity, we'd have to be responsible for gathering firewood to heat the house in winter, we would have to take on regular and ongoing maintenance issues, and so on. By no means would we call our changes drastic, or even uncomfortable; yet many of our contemporaries would see such a lifestyle as an impossible sacrifice.

In 1968 geneticist Garrett Hardin wrote an article entitled "The Tragedy of the Commons," in which he argued that unmanaged access to common resources resulted in a lawless and unethical future. He illustrated this human tendency toward greed by giving an example of a herdsman who is faced with the temptations of a common pasture. The herdsman will instinctively overload it with his livestock. Likewise, as each greed-driven human tries to maximize resources for personal gain, the common resources collapse to the detriment of all.

Such a bleak portrait of the decline of the earth's "pastures" certainly seems to be happening in many places today. "Good-tasting water is going to disappear," my mother said so long ago. "One day people will have to pay a lot of money for a drink." Now water, life's most precious common resource, is being sold like soda pop; it fills an entire isle of my local chain grocery store. Privatization of resources gives corporations sole access to what was once held in common by humans, while it lays the ill health and environmental costs on society.

But Hardin's tragic parable of a lawless, unethical future was only if the commons were *unmanaged*. A managed commons, though it may have other problems, will not automatically suffer the tragic fate of the unmanaged commons. Taxes, regulations, strict laws, and other restraints must be placed to prevent corporations from depleting our resources.

If a handful of private corporations continue to monopolize the earth's resources, while common people bear the ever-increasing costs, more and more social protests will arise into violent protest of that imbalance. "The threat to our future is not from greedy individuals," Hardin wrote, "but from unregulated voracious emissaries who have no respect for limits, and no sustainable, inclusive vision of what it means, long term, to belong."

If sustainability is defined simply as maintaining the status quo, we are dreaming. We should make political and personal choices to reduce the human ecological footprint—*not* in order to regain some pastoral vision of an open horizon of endless possibilities but in self-defense against a chaotic and constantly changing environment. We don't need to *sustain* what we have; rather, we need to provide ourselves with as many options for the future as possible: choices for keeping warm, choices for powering our devices, choices for ensuring the interdependence of all beings.

11. Aunt Ora

Ora Orme was born in Arizona around 1885 and was raised on a large ranch of cacti and tumbleweeds. She never married. She lived in various places around the Southwest with her childhood friend Marie and eventually settled in Tesuque, New Mexico. She was the great-aunt of the people who put me up while I was teaching there, and she lived in their house with them.

She was in her nineties when I lived there, and had great difficulty moving around. But she was sharp as a tack and tough as nails. Aunt Ora had once been a teacher and took great interest in the Tesuque school. She knew all about the school: the political situation that created it, the unusual curriculum, the outdoor classrooms, and—simply by the fact that a long-haired baby of twenty-two was living in her house—the people who were teaching there.

One afternoon, a teacher's meeting was to be held at the house. Aunt Ora was sitting in the living room while I was waiting for the other teachers to arrive. I had not had much conversation with her, and I stumbled with the awkwardness of youth.

"I understand you were a school teacher once."

"Yes," she said, "yes, I was."

"Where did you teach?"

"I taught in Arizona," she said, fingering an afghan that covered the chair in which she sat. "My friend Marie and I both taught there. It was in 1921 or thereabouts . . ."

"What was it like?"

"The school was twenty miles from Mammoth, Arizona. Out on the desert. The children had to come from many, many miles. It was different back then for a teacher, different than today's schools. Maybe more like the school you have here in Tesuque."

I didn't say anything. She looked off into some distant place and then continued.

"It was just Marie and me and about fifty children. We each taught everything, but Marie also taught music. That was her specialty. Oh, and she was good at it. Those kids loved to sing; we even had a small brass band.

"We didn't have grade levels. We just had two classrooms and no grades. Marie took half the children, and I took the other half. We taught them all the regular things—their reading and writing and how to do their figures . . . but we also taught them . . ."

"What Aunt Ora?"

"Well, we also taught them how to live. I mean . . . when they left, those children knew something about the world, and they knew something about themselves. All of them were born in the area, and most of them would probably die there. So we taught them about the world by teaching them about the desert. They learned about the rocks and plants and so on. They learned all of that, but they also learned . . . oh dear, they learned *respect*. Respect for the desert and respect for the world and respect for each other. They grew up some at our school, not by what Marie and I taught them—we could only teach them so much—but because of what they learned from each other. We made sure they learned about each other and about respect."

Then she turned to me. "Tell me about you," she said.

I started talking about myself, and before long I grew full of youthful pride. "And I am a conscientious objector," I said. "I'm against the war in Vietnam."

"You're a what?" Aunt Ora asked.

"I'm a conscientious objector. I just don't think killing other people is the way to solve problems," I said.

"You mean you aren't willing to defend this country?" She rolled her head toward me and squinted. "Tell me that. What about this country?"

"It's just that I think I could do more good for the country by staying out of the war and working with the kids here, teaching at Tesuque."

"Ah," she said, and then leaned back. "Why yes. Yes. Yes."

III. Another Artifact

William Cade was an eighteen-year-old resident of Barnet, Vermont, when he enlisted in the Union army in July 1862. Recently, when a donor gave the town's historical society his diary, I volunteered to help transcribe it.

Two months after he enlisted, he wrote his first diary entry, reporting that his regiment marched from Washington DC to Arlington Heights, Virginia. In these earliest entries his comments are short, as he records only the most fundamental elements of his day: his location, travel, and a word or two about his activities. Initially he also kept careful track of money he loaned to friends, meticulously crossing out the debt, presumably when it had been paid.

These financial records soon all but disappear in place of more a personal tone. As time passes, his entries become longer and more detailed, with names of fellow soldiers, specifics of his duties, and taut comments about battles. He records letters he wrote to his parents, relatives, and friends back home in Barnet, as well as the dozens and dozens he wrote "to Emma."

The great bulk of the diary reports the tedious hard work of camp life or the simple details of grueling marches:

"We drew three days ration, was told it had to last for 5."

"Marched about 25 miles, and camped after dark."

"We lay in camp all day and it rained so hard there was no fighting at all today so we lay in camp all night."

Without comment, he records the details of the day-to-day tensions that arose in the heat of battle, or of being drawn up in the line of battle, only to return to camp:

"We found that the Rebs are not going to attack us here, so they have fallen back to try the thing over. But I emma fraid they are not done yet."

"We camped in the battle field where there was a few with their legs shot off, but they was all dead."

He likely felt compelled to keep his comments short enough that they would fit in the space provided for the date in the printed diary. He almost never exceeds that limit; and when he does, he squeezes only a few final words into the margin.

Even without the harrowing five final months of his entries, the Cade diary still would provide an evocative sketch of the life of a young New England soldier. But what makes his record so compelling is that we are witness to the painful final months of a young man's life.

On June 1, 1863, less than two years after he enlisted, William Cade was shot through the hips at the battle of Cold Harbor, Virginia. For the next five months, as he lay dying, he stoically recorded his pain and suffering. His wounds oozed puss; and several times a day and in the middle of the night, blood poured from his rectum. Still, he writes without comment except to report those simple facts and then adds a report of the weather for that day.

For three months, he was kept at a Washington DC hospital, until September, when he was finally taken to a hospital in Montpelier, Vermont, fifty miles from his hometown. For a brief day or two his spirits seem to brighten as he claims he feels a little better, but soon the entries become more and more sparse.

"My wounds run hard ..." "Cramps. I can't help myself enny ..." "No better today. Wounds run bad. Sunny and pleasant ..."

His parents visit him, as does a friend's father and a fellow soldier "quite smartly dressed." But the litany never ceases:

"Bowels are held outside, not inside."

"In Grate pain, my legs can't move enny."

"Cramped up and I can't help myself."

"My legs cant move."

Finally, at the end of October, the handwriting in the diary changes—someone else is writing his words. Only then are we allowed to hear his suffering, and then only in snippets: "Oh God is there no rest for me." And then, finally, the day before the last entry: "O may God free me from my pain!" Two days later, on November 2, 1863, William Cade was dead.

He was twenty years old.

IV. The Rocking Chair

On one side of our vegetable garden sits an old, wooden rocking chair. The ancient chair is in too poor a shape to sit in. The rockers are missing, and one of the armrests hangs from the frame, broken and bent. In summer we simply put a pot of geraniums on the seat and use it as a slowly deteriorating lawn ornament.

The rocking chair was already ancient when I bought it in high school. I found it at a yard sale and immediately fell in love with it. I decided it would fit in my small bedroom and make a great alternative to sitting on my bed or on the hard, wooden chair where I sat to do my homework. I debated for only a short while before I forked over the hefty sum of $10 and hauled it away.

When I bought the rocking chair, its padded seat was made of leather, a horsehair-filled cushion that sat on a set of box springs. Shortly after I bought it and as a surprise gift to me, my parents refurbished the chair. Dad removed the old seat and replaced it with a sturdy platform, while my mother used her sewing skills to replace the old cushion with a comfortable pillow. My father made some repairs to the frame, and Mom stained the wood to a deep, luxurious brown.

When I moved into the yurt, I found that it would not fit through the narrow door, so I set the rocking chair down just outside, where it served as a comfortable spot to sit and read, shaded from the afternoon sunlight by the yurt itself. Those rare times when I had visitors, I dragged it to the fire pit so that my guest could sit and enjoy the evening.

After I left the yurt, the rocking chair became domestic again, following me from one dwelling to another; but its time outside in the desert had weathered the old wood and weakened it. Over the years, I have repaired its joints, glued and fastened and fixed its frame, and replaced my mother's sewn seat cover. I've read a library's worth of books in that old chair and rocked each of my infant sons to sleep with its motion, but finally not even my patchwork repairs could save it. Still, I couldn't bear to throw it away.

When we moved into the straw bale house, I left it outside next to the fire pit we use for summer barbeques. For a little while longer you could still sit in the thing and even feel the gentle sway of the old rockers, but soon even that became impossible.

Now, as I said, it sits out its final days beyond the garden, still useful as a planter and as a perch for the phoebes as they wait, watching, for another insect meal. I bought that rocker for what I believed was an extravagant price: the ten bucks I spent on it was nearly a full day's earnings. I never imagined that it would remain useful to me for a lifetime.

Like that chair, my experiences at trying to live in closer harmony with the people and places around me have served me in ways I never expected. I am often asked if I think I made the right decision to build the straw bale or if my time on the desert was simply wasted. How can I answer, for to do so would mean I could have foreseen the future and all the complicated, unpredictable consequences of its unfolding. What I can tell you is that both experiences taught me that no one has to spend life's precious resources of time and money, of healthy air and clean water, in order to live a full and rich life. Building the straw bale and the yurt showed me that I can simplify my life. I can reduce my needs to the most basic—food and shelter—and, in doing so, increase one thousand-fold the intricate rewards of living an examined life.

v. Sustainable Compromises

"Every hippie's dream," someone once called my sojourn at the yurt, but it was no dream: we could have changed the world.

The great writer and prankster Ken Kesey said that people in the 1960s and '70s understood we had to consider new ways for things to be; people understood that all beings are one. "The deeper I got into it, the more I realized there was a different force working," he said. "The only big mistake we ever made as a force was thinking for a while that we were going to win." He said that soon people developed vested interests in the victory to come, so now "we parcel off into little groups, whether it's feminism, or politics, money, or religion, whatever it is, everyone is jumping up and down in front of it, until nobody can see it clear anymore."

We must stop jumping up and down and once again see how life depends on the interdependence of all things. The only way to do so is to confront the pollution of our own consciousness.

As the gypsy who read my palm understood, steadfast allegiance to our unquestioned ideals cannot make a viable future. We must constantly reevaluate our beliefs and adapt ourselves to meet the ever-changing conditions before us.

We must learn to find compromise in ourselves, in our religions, and in our wars. We must peel back the possessiveness of our own beliefs, our own righteous indignation, and seek peace within ourselves. For that, there can be no sustainable compromise.

vi. Becoming

"Power ceases in the instant of repose," wrote Ralph Waldo Emerson. "It resides in the moment of transition from a past to a new state, in the shooting of the gulf, in the darting to an aim. This one fact the world hates, that the soul *becomes*, for that forever degrades the past, turns all riches to poverty, all reputations to a shame, confounds the saint with the rogue, shoves Jesus and Judas aside equally."

We may despise how everything changes; but when we cling to an image created in the past, it limits our future. To sustain life, we must accept that change is a fundamental feature of all natural systems. I must accept my life's mistakes and constantly turn my attention to the work that needs to be done.

20

- - - - - - - - -

Postscript

Mistakes Were Made

While researching before we built the straw bale house, I came on an article on the Internet entitled "Build a House in Two Days Using Straw." It gave me a good laugh.

The first mistake I made was thinking that a man approaching sixty could take on a three-year-long project that would challenge a strong and able-bodied man in his twenties. It was tough on both body and soul.

Aside from the many aches and pains I've already complained about, there are other things I would do differently if I had the chance.

Because of the concrete floor and the solid walls, sounds travel easily in the new house. It's hard for one person to be on the phone while the other is doing anything that requires quiet. Throw rugs help; but because the bare floor is a critical part of the efficiency of the house, we don't want to cover it too much. Lower ceilings in some parts of the house would help, and one possible home improvement project already under consideration is lowering the ceiling a bit in the more intimate areas of the house.

Likewise, I wish I had designed a way to incorporate shutters on the large, south-facing windows. The way it is now, in order to keep nice warm air from radiating back outside on long winter nights, we use drapes over the windows. We take them entirely off during the days in order to get the maximum heat of the winter sun. The drapes are a hassle and not nearly as efficient as carefully constructed and designed shutters would have been.

Also, I wish I had been more careful with my body. I smoked tobacco while I lived at the yurt, for example, puffing the foul stuff through the mandatory famous-writer's pipe. I gave that up a long time ago, but did I learn? While building the straw bale, I constantly failed to protect my lungs or my ears from the noise and the toxins involved.

While I understood that living in an alternative house would require unusual and consistent maintenance, I did not fully appreciate how doing so might become increasingly challenging as I grew older. Shortly before our decision to build, a handful of fellow Amoebans looked into the possibility of buying a large house, fixing it up, and living there collectively. The plan fizzled out, but such a collective and intentional community would have eased the solitary responsibilities that come with a house just for two of us.

While being off grid means that we save money and use fewer resources, the batteries for our solar power will wear out and will need to be replaced. The production of deep-cell batteries, to say nothing of the ecological consequences of disposing of used batteries, has an impact on the environment. Buying new batteries will also be an expense, and we have had to budget to put aside money for when that becomes necessary. This also means we are not absolutely independent from using the earth's limited resources or immune to the fluctuation of world markets.

Ultimately the cost of building a straw bale house is not much different than that of a conventionally built wood-frame house. In most areas the bales can be purchased cheaply from local farmers, and since using straw is owner-as-builder friendly, there are some savings possible. However, the cost of additional labor for

Fig. 14. The finished house from the south

working with the straw, and the basic costs that are necessary for any house construction, means that a straw bale house is probably only slightly less expensive than a house built with traditional materials. Since I did a lot of the work by myself, or with the seemingly inexhaustible supply of friends, we were able to build our house for roughly $109 a square foot. That probably was not much different than the cost of a similarly built standard house with two-by-six framing with R-19 insulated walls. The difference, of course, is that our walls are far superior in terms of comfort, efficiency, and aesthetics.

But we were just as stupid as a lot of other people when we gambled that the housing market would remain so vibrant. Our near financial disaster was brought about because we expected the future to be an extension of the immediate past. To be better prepared for the unknown, we should have left ourselves more options.

Thoreau's cabin isn't just a home; it's a moral statement that there is a better way to live. While he said that everyone needs to find her or his *own* way of life, he did get downright preachy about the excesses he saw in conventional society.

Fig. 15. The finished house from the north

Likewise, a reader might assume I claim that I built my house "the right way"—that building an off-grid straw bale house is somehow superior to any other kind of home. My home is not perfect and, lord knows, neither is the builder, but our house is *somewhat* more efficient, *somewhat* cheaper to own, *somewhat* more sustainable than a traditional house.

When I lived at the yurt, I burned what little trash I generated in a large barrel. I knew it smelled of chemicals and pollution, but I burned it anyway, watching the blue smoke as if it were some weird ceremonial fire. I should have known better. The mistake was not in the burning but in my disregard of the larger consequences of my actions.

In spite of the problems that have arisen, the mistakes I have made, and the anguish I endured while building them, both the yurt and the straw bale have given me an opportunity to live what Socrates called an "examined life," in ways a more traditional life would have made impossible.

When I wandered the desert around the yurt, I purposefully left one large section unexplored. I wanted to leave it forever unknown,

I told myself, to retain the sense of mystery in my life. And so it is that some regions of our own psyche should remain forever unexplored, just as parts of our own surroundings should always remain uncharted and unknown, tantalizing us with the mystery of their being.

Yesterday I walked my land, looking for an invasive plant called Japanese knotweed. The World Conservation Union has listed the plant as one of the world's worst invasive species, and it is widespread in Vermont. Once established, it becomes so densely packed that it creates a monoculture, where no other plant life can grow.

The hollow stems of the plant look like bamboo, and it grows in almost any soil. It can survive temperatures to forty below and is nearly impossible to eradicate. Cut it down and it regenerates twice as thick from the roots. Dig up the thick network of roots if you can, but they form clusters that are ten feet deep and twenty-five feet wide. Plus, the roots regenerate so easily that it is difficult to dispose of them.

The only way to get rid of the plant is to kill the roots. So far, the most common way of doing this is to treat the plants with an herbicide, like the commercial product Round-Up. The most sustainable way of getting rid of the plants, yet not the most easily accomplished, is by injecting steam into the roots in order to kill them.

I have not yet found any Japanese knotweed on my land, but it'll be here soon enough. Then I will have to decide just what to do with it. Perhaps we are fighting a losing battle over such species. On a well-traveled Vermont highway, someone has placed a large, homemade sign against a backdrop of forest. The simple truth may be the words of that sign. It reads, "Evolution or Extinction."

Maybe our "mistake" is the idea of sustainability itself, as if we can sustain something that is always in flux—a flux made more rapid by our own contribution. Instead of trying to sustain our little niche, we need to develop an environmental awareness to give us more options against an unknown and rapidly changing future.

I sat in the idling car, the relentless drizzling snow of the endless winter slashing on the hood. I sat in the silence of that pounding while trying on and then letting go of words: I lingered on words of hope—what Emily Dickinson called the thing with feathers—too wrapped in the moment to dare whisper them, lest by simply speaking of a hopeful future, I condemned it to dreamland.

I contemplated my own tenuous place in the world, untethered and about to step forward into the unknown. I shuddered then, recognizing how easily it all passes, "like taking scissors to a string," says Dylan. First a spring morning in the sun of a youthful desert, in deep joy, love, and understanding, and then that thing with feathers has flown. Autumn returns, and then the darkness again.

But tonight, as I sat in the warming car, none of those darker words formed on my lips. Tonight there was the speechless grasping that this moment, stolen and rushed—this moment was real: I must meet the future with kindness and generosity. The others here beside me are nothing but my own being.

Acknowledgments

_ _ _ _ _ _ _ _ _ _

The All-Around Everything Masters without Whom There Wouldn't Be a House or a Book: Rick Stodola, Jon Fitch, Richard Moye, Tom Robinson, Alan Fogg, and Bob Gross. Bridget Barry, Sabrina Ehmke Sergeant, and Linda Wacholder.

Hammers, Brooms, Brushes, Sweat, Tears, Color Consultation, and Marital Therapists: Sherri Fitch, Barb Wacholder, John Ajamie, Elaine Robinson, Vicki Litzinger, Susan Ohlidal, Greg Dinkel, Buck Beliles, Meri Simon, Kathy Bales, Len Gerardi, Cathy Ajamie, Lauren Moye, Lauren Jarvi, Jeff Briggs, Paula Briggs, Rob Hoppe, Kris Hoppe, Jessie Tidyman, and Dan Primmer.

Berry Turnovers, Bean Enchiladas, Spinach Casseroles, More Endless Great Food, Good Cheer, and Encouragement a Thousand Hours Deep: Trish Pennypacker.

Special Angel at Critical Moments Award: Jeff Gutt.

Helped Not Just Because It's Their Inheritance: Andrew Boye, Ben Boye, and John Boye.

BEST Samaritan Award: Norm and Linda Dagnaut.

Straw Movers: the Kozlowski brothers.

Advice, Kindness, Straw Storage and Transport, and Support: Dave Conant, Rod Zwick, Chad Pennypacker, Dave Lenton, Henri Lenton, Tim McKay, Betsy McKay, and Gordon Goss.

It Takes a Village Participants: David Beliles, Jessica Beliles, Bill Price, Claire Stodola, Luke Stodola, Nathan Stodola, Amy Stodola, Cathy Russell, Alan Rowe, Dave Plazek, Tina Plazek, "Gangsta" Andrew Bilir-Flock, Gavin Thurston, Jake Styles, Wally Sophrin,

Lauren Sophrin, Jordan Grove, Heather Keith, Steve Fessmere, David Boye, Kristin Brooks, Dylan Ford, Bobby Farlice-Rubio, Tyler McGill, Jonah Tidyman, Jeremy Brown, and Ryan Mesch.

For Always Saving Me a Seat on the Bus: Dawn Madore.

Construction Materials, Good Advice, Great Help: Allen Lumber, St. Jay Hardware. *Deep Well and Good Water:* John Ainsworth Water Systems. *Plumbing Materials:* F. W. Webb Co.—especially Dick and Donny—and Appalachian Supply Co. *Gas Plumbing:* Lloyd Rowell. *Concrete Foundation, Floor, and Acid Stain:* Lunnie Concrete, especially Harold Lunnie and crew. *Concrete Supplies:* Hopkins & Sons. *Straw Bale Construction:* GreenSpace Collaborative, especially Andy Mueller and crew. *Solar Power:* Independent Power, especially Dave Palumbo and crew. *Excavation, Advice, and Good Humor:* Dan Thompson and crew. *Chimney:* Gary Nelson. *Septic Design:* Keith Johnson. *Custom Windows:* Mayo's Glass. *Recycled Materials and Inspiration:* Admac Salvage. *Banking and Financial:* Passumpsic Savings Bank, especially Cathy Clark. *Stained Glass:* League of NH Craftspersons.

Inspiration: My students from *Las Tres Villas* and those from the "Walden Class" everywhere.

Faith and Decades of Support: Lyndon State College.

A Residency of Solitude, Space, and Time for the Writing of this Book: the Ragdale Foundation.

Notes

– – – – – – – – – –

1. What I Lived For

The average cost for new homes in the United States can be found online at U.S. Bureau of the Census, "Median and Average Sales Prices of New Homes Sold in United States," U.S. Census Bureau, accessed July 18, 2013, http://www.census.gov/const /uspriceann.pdf.

For yurt resources, see Yurt Info's website at http://www.yurtinfo .org/, accessed July 18, 2013.

2. Sustainable Compromises

For the Vermont Septic Law, see State of Vermont, "Wastewater System and Potable Water Supply Rules," chap. 1, State of Vermont Environmental Protection Rules (effective September 29, 2007).

4. Water

Regarding hyperobjects, see also Nixon, *Slow Violence and the Environmentalism of the Poor.*

For the map of Vermont water wells, see Vermont Department of Environmental Conservation, "Statewide Groundwater Analyses," accessed July 24, 2013.

For a sample water budget, see "Water Budget," *Sustainable Sources: 19 Years of Online Green Building Information*, accessed July 24, 2013, http://waterbudget.sustainablesources.com.

5. Design

Energy use and carbon dioxide emissions regarding concrete are from "Cement and Concrete."

For more on the history of straw bale construction, see Welsch, "Baled Hay."

For photographs of the oldest straw bale buildings, see "A Photo Tour of Nebraska's Straw-Bale Buildings," *The Last Straw: The International Quarterly Journal of Straw Bale and Natural Building*, accessed July 18, 2013, http://thelaststraw.org/sban/tour/tour.html.

For an example of the Eye design, see "1800 Sq. Ft. (Eye)," Balewatch.com, accessed July 18, 2013, http://www.balewatch.com/1800.eye.html.

6. Foundations

Some of my information about Earth People's Park is from "Earth People's Park," *Wikipedia*, last modified February 12, 2013, http://en.wikipedia.org/wiki/Earth_Peoples_Park.

7. El Sol

For solar radiation statistics, see the National Solar Radiation Data Base, 1961–1990, found online at http://rredc.nrel.gov/solar/old_data/nsrdb/1961-1990/, accessed July 24, 2013.

8. Economics

The quotes from Thich Nhat Hanh are from *Essential Writings*, p. 69.

10. The Amoeba

For information about the effect of industrialization on the sense of community, I am indebted to Gross, "'That Terrible Thoreau.'"

11. The Straw That Broke The

The etymology of the word "straw" is from the *Oxford English Dictionary*.

The history of the drinking straw is from Thompson, "Invention of the Bendy Straw."

12. Finances

For a summary of the oil crisis of 1973, see Regional Oral History Office, "1973–74 Oil Crisis," accessed July 24, 2013.

13. Collaboration

Information about the closing of the Tesuque school is from newspaper articles in the author's private collection.

17. Thick Skin in a Winter of Discontent

For the Rajneesh/Osho comments on euthanasia and genetic selection, see "Vision: The Greatest Challenge: the Golden Future," *Osho Times Online*, accessed July 18, 2013, http://www.osho.com /magazine/oshointro/visiongoldenindexdetails.cfm?Golden=birth.

Additional information regarding the Rajneesh movement is from McCormack, *Oregon Magazine*, see especially p. 114.

18. Spring

For more on the Anasazi search for the center, see "Glyph Time" in my *Tales from the Journey of the Dead*.

19. Higher Laws

For the threat posed by unregulated corporations, see Nixon, "Neoliberalism, Genre and 'The Tragedy of the Commons.'"

Emerson's quote is from p. 29, *Self-Reliance and Other Essays* (Dover, Mineola NY, 1993).

Kesey's quote is from Gibney and Ellwood, *Magic Trip*.

Bibliography

— — — — — — — —

Abbey, Edward. *Desert Solitaire: A Season in the Wilderness.* New York: Dial Press, 1962.

Ackerman, Diane. "The Brain on Love." *New York Times*, March 25, 2012.

Bhanoo, Sindya N. "The Battle over Bottled Water." *Green: A Blog about Energy and the Environment*, March 24, 2010. http://green.blogs.nytimes .com/2010/03/24/the-battle-over-bottled-water/.

Blackman, Allan. *Face to Face with Your Draft Board.* Berkeley CA: World without War Council, 1969.

Boye, Alan. *Tales from the Journey of the Dead: Ten Thousand Years on an American Desert.* Lincoln: University of Nebraska Press, 2004.

———. *The Complete Roadside Guide to Nebraska.* 2nd ed. Lincoln: Bison, 2007.

"Cement and Concrete: Environmental Considerations." *Environmental Building News* 2, no. 2 (1993): 1–12.

Chiras, Daniel D. *The Solar House: Passive Heating and Cooling.* White River Junction VT: Chelsea Green, 2002.

Clark, Sam. *Independent Builder: Designing and Building a House Your Own Way.* White River Junction VT: Chelsea Green, 1996.

Day, Dorothy. "Transcendence." *Catholic Worker* 73, no. 6 (2006): 1.

Emerson, Ralph Waldo. *Self-Reliance and Other Essays.* Mineola NY: Dover, 1993.

Gandhi, Mohandas. *The Essential Gandhi: An Anthology of His Writings on His Life, Work and Ideas.* Edited by Louis Fischer. New York: Vintage, 2002.

Garcia Marquez, Gabriel. *One Hundred Years of Solitude.* Harper Perennial Modern Classics edition. New York: Harper Perennial, 2006. First published under the title *Cien Años de Soledad* in 1967 by Editorial Sudamericanos.

George, Rose. *The Big Necessity: The Unmentionable World of Human Waste and Why It Matters.* New York: Metropolitan, 2008.

Gibney, Alex, and Allison Ellwood. *Magic Trip: Ken Kesey's Search for a Kool Place.* New York: History Chanel Films, 2011. Distributed by Magnolia Pictures. DVD, 90 min.

Gross, Robert A. "'That Terrible Thoreau': Concord and Its Hermit." In *A Historical Guide to Henry David Thoreau*, edited by William E. Cain, 192–193. Oxford: Oxford University Press, 2002.

Hardin, Garrett. "The Tragedy of the Commons." *Science* 162, no. 3859 (1968): 1243–48.

Jerilou, Hammett, Kingsley Hammett, and Peter Scholz. *The Essence of Santa Fe: From a Way of Life to a Style.* Santa Fe: Ancient City Press, 2006.

Kachadorian, James. *The Passive Solar House: Using Solar Design to Heat and Cool Your Home.* White River Junction VT: Chelsea Green, 1997.

Lacinski, Paul, and Michael Bergeron. *Serious Straw Bale: A Home Construction Guide for All Climates.* White River Junction VT: Chelsea Green, 2000.

Leopold, Aldo. *Sand County Almanac.* Oxford: Oxford University Press, 1966.

Magwood, Chris, Peter Mack, and Tima Therrien. *More Straw Bale Building: A Complete Guide to Designing and Building with Straw.* Gabriola Island BC: New Society Publishers, 2005.

McCormack, Win, ed. *Oregon Magazine: The Rajneesh Files, 1981–86.* Salem: New Oregon Press, 1985.

McDonough, William, and Michael Braungart. *Cradle to Cradle: Remaking the Way We Make Things.* New York: North Point, 2002.

Merton, Thomas. *Thoughts in Solitude.* New York: Farrar, Straus, and Giroux, 1999.

Morton, Timothy. "Hyperobjects and the End of Common Sense." *The Contemporary Condition* (blog), March 18, 2010. http://contemporarycondition .blogspot.com/2010/03/hyperobjects-and-end-of-common-sense.html.

Nhat Hanh, Thich. *Essential Writings.* Maryknoll NY: Orbis, 2001.

Nixon, Rob. "Neoliberalism, Genre and 'The Tragedy of the Commons.'" *PMLA* 127, no. 3 (2012): 598–99.

———. *Slow Violence and the Environmentalism of the Poor.* Boston: Harvard University Press, 2011.

Owens, Ted. *Building with Awareness: The Construction of a Hybrid Home.* Corrales NM: Syncronos Design, 2005.

Photovoltaics: Design and Installation Manual. Carbondale CO: Solar Energy International, 2004.

Regional Oral History Office. "1973–74 Oil Crisis." *Slaying the Dragon of Debt.* Berkeley: University of California, Berkeley, 2011. Found online at http:// bancroft.berkeley.edu/ROHO/projects/debt/oilcrisis.html.

Schaeffer, Jack. *Monte Walsh.* Lincoln: Bison, 2003.

———. *Shane: The Critical Edition.* Edited by James C. Work. Lincoln: University of Nebraska Press, 1984.

Schaeffer, John. *Real Goods Solar Living Source Book: Your Complete Guide to Renewable Energy Technologies and Sustainable Living.* 12th ed. White River Junction VT: Chelsea Green, 2006.

Seney, Noel, and Larry Clayton, eds. *Better Homes and Gardens Step-by-Step Basic Wiring.* Des Moines IA: Meredith, 1980.

Spence, William P. *Carpentry and Building Construction: A Do-it-Yourself Guide.* New York: Sterling, 1995.

Steen, Athena Swentzell, Bill Steen, David Bainbridge, and David Eisenberg. *The Straw Bale House.* White River Junction VT: Chelsea Green, 1994.

The Last Straw: The International Quarterly Journal of Straw Bale and Natural Building. Editor: Joyce Coppinger. Lincoln NE: Green Prairie Foundation for Sustainability, 1993–, various issues.

Thompson, Derek. "The Amazing History and the Strange Invention of the Bendy Straw." *Atlantic,* November 22, 2011. http://www.theatlantic .com/business/archive/2011/11/the-amazing-history-and-the-strange -invention-of-the-bendy-straw/248923/.

Thoreau, Henry David. *Walden; or, Life in the Woods.* Mineola NY: Dover, 1995.

Ueshiba, Morihei. *The Art of Peace.* Translated by John Stevens. Boston: Shambhala, 2002.

Vermont Department of Environmental Conservation. "Statewide Ground-water Analyses." *Vermont Geological Survey,* 2008. http://www.anr.state .vt.us/dec/geo/gwaterSTATEinx.htm.

Wanek, Catherine. *The New Strawbale Home.* Layton UT: Gibbs Smith, 2005.

Watson, Donald. *Designing and Building a Solar House: Your Place in the Sun.* Charlotte VT: Garden Way, 1977.

Welsch, Roger. "Baled Hay." In *Shelter,* 70–71. Bolinas CA: Shelter Publications, 1974.

In the Our Sustainable Future series

Ogallala: Water for a Dry Land
John Opie

Building Soils for Better Crops: Organic Matter Management
Fred Magdoff

Agricultural Research Alternatives
William Lockeretz and Molly D. Anderson

Crop Improvement for Sustainable Agriculture
Edited by M. Brett Callaway and Charles A. Francis

Future Harvest: Pesticide-Free Farming
Jim Bender

*A Conspiracy of Optimism: Management of the National Forests
since World War Two*
Paul W. Hirt

Green Plans: Greenprint for Sustainability
Huey D. Johnson

Making Nature, Shaping Culture: Plant Biodiversity in Global Context
Lawrence Busch, William B. Lacy, Jeffrey Burkhardt, Douglas Hemken,
Jubel Moraga-Rojel, Timothy Koponen, and José de Souza Silva

Economic Thresholds for Integrated Pest Management
Edited by Leon G. Higley and Larry P. Pedigo

Ecology and Economics of the Great Plains
Daniel S. Licht

Uphill against Water: The Great Dakota Water War
Peter Carrels

*Changing the Way America Farms: Knowledge and Community in the Sustainable
Agriculture Movement*
Neva Hassanein

Ogallala: Water for a Dry Land, second edition
John Opie

Willard Cochrane and the American Family Farm
Richard A. Levins

Down and Out on the Family Farm: Rural Rehabilitation
in the Great Plains, 1929-1945
Michael Johnston Grant

Raising a Stink: The Struggle over Factory Hog Farms in Nebraska
Carolyn Johnsen

The Curse of American Agricultural Abundance: A Sustainable Solution
Willard W. Cochrane

Good Growing: Why Organic Farming Works
Leslie A. Duram

Roots of Change: Nebraska's New Agriculture
Mary Ridder

Remaking American Communities: A Reference Guide to Urban Sprawl
Edited by David C. Soule
Foreword by Neal Peirce

Remaking the North American Food System: Strategies for Sustainability
Edited by C. Clare Hinrichs and Thomas A. Lyson

Crisis and Opportunity: Sustainability in American Agriculture
John E. Ikerd

Green Plans: Blueprint for a Sustainable Earth, revised and updated
Huey D. Johnson

Green Illusions: The Dirty Secrets of Clean Energy and
the Future of Environmentalism
Ozzie Zehner

Traveling the Power Line: From the Mojave Desert to the Bay of Fundy
Julianne Couch

Sustainable Compromises: A Yurt, A Straw Bale House, and Ecological Living
Alan Boye

To order or obtain more information on these or other University of Nebraska Press
titles, visit nebraskapress.unl.edu.